The Rosy Future of War

Philippe Delmas

THE FREE PRESS

New York   London   Toronto   Sydney   Singapore

Translation by Christopher Atamian
Revised Translation by Camilla Hewitt

THE FREE PRESS
A Division of Simon & Schuster Inc.
1230 Avenue of the Americas
New York, NY 10020

French language edition first published in France as
Le Bel Avenir de la guerre by Éditions Gallimard

THE FREE PRESS and colophon are trademarks
of Simon & Schuster Inc.

Designed by Carla Bolte

Manufactured in the United States of America

10   9   8   7   6   5   4   3   2   1

Library of Congress Cataloging-in-Publication Data

Delmas, Philippe.
     [Bel avenir de la guerre. English]
     The rosy future of war / Philippe Delmas.
          p.   cm.
     Includes bibliographical references.
     ISBN 0–684–83370–0
     1. Political stability.   2. War.   3. World politics—1989–
I. Title.
JC330.2.D4513   1997
320.9′049—dc21   97-4177
                                              CIP

WAR IS THE PROVINCE OF LIFE AND DEATH

—Sun Tzu

To my parents

In honor of their wisdom and their unshakable

courage

Contents

The Rosy Future of War

CHAPTER 1

Order Without Peace?

Nothing is more difficult to overcome than the problems
we thought were already overcome.

—Alexis de Tocqueville

Order Without Peace?

Can peace be guaranteed? The question seems almost ridiculous,
so much is human history the history of war. In the last twenty-five
centuries of its history, China has known only two centuries of
peace. In the twenty centuries of our history in the West, we have
done no better. Civilization has been unable to overcome war; in
fact the regulating of relationships between powers comes down
regulating the waging of wars between them. Nothing about war
has been reduced except the actual number of powers able to wage
it. In the Middle Ages, any petty noble could declare war on another. As the centuries have passed, the power to declare and to
wage war has become the sole right of sovereign States, and of
fewer and fewer of those. Meanwhile those same States invented
and defined the concept of "order," meaning not social harmony
but the suppression of any activity unacceptable to the State. The
"order" that held States together until recently was not peace but a
list of justifications for declaring war: sovereignty, borders, vital interests. A country's power was measured by its ability to participate
in maintaining an international order in which its own interests
were respected by other countries.

This international order fostered stability, but not peace. For the true advantage of the great powers was their ability to provoke or to end wars among other, lesser powers. War occurred among the great powers themselves only when a previously established order was violated or when another country's expansion was too threatening to it. Thus in 1815 the great powers of Europe, meeting at the Congress of Vienna, negotiated the end of the wars unleashed by the French Revolution twenty-five years earlier. Borders were redrawn and a new international order was established in Europe that endured for the next fifty years. This order was destroyed in 1866 when Prussia, deciding that those borders were no longer to its liking, successfully waged war on Europe for the next five years. In the interim, between 1815 and 1866, while the European powers were enjoying peace at home, they started wars abroad: in China, Mexico, the Crimea, and Africa. . . .

The logic that keeps such an international order in place is as old as wars and States themselves. Over the centuries, it became more subtle and complicated but its basic character never changed. Its imperatives spread to affect more and more countries until finally the whole planet was under its sway. This globalization of the international order meant that fewer and fewer States were able to take an active part in defining it, because more and more power was needed to do so. Finally the few remaining great world powers became completely polarized in the Cold War. The five countries that officially possessed the nuclear bomb were set apart from all the other nations of the world. The bomb's enormous power made the maintenance of the international order an absolute necessity: to violate it meant not only war but global death. This ultimate threat raised the stakes in the world order as high as they could possibly go, but did not change its basic nature. On the contrary, traditional concepts like vital interests and balances of power became more intensely held than ever; whereas before they were considered merely aspects of strategy, they were now felt to be ideological, even theological in their importance.

At a basic level, however, things stayed about the same. Since war among themselves was now impossible, the world powers waged it elsewhere, and with increased ferocity. There was no such thing as "nuclear peace." Wars actually continued everywhere—only *nuclear* war was averted.

This order is now a thing of the past, but we still know what it was like. It gives us much to think about because the world-wide awareness of the threat of nuclear annihilation is the only such world-wide awareness that mankind has ever known. That mutual assured nuclear destruction stands as the only guarantee of peace in the history of man clearly shows us how much work has to be done if we are ever to learn how to live in peace together. . . . The more we uncover what that nuclear-based order was really all about, however, the more we realize that it will have no successor; no accord or treaty will ever replace the certainty of death as the ultimate deterrent to war. For a short time after the Cold War ended, we thought we could make it into a true peace. But no diplomatic convention, no format of treaty (like those of which history has seen so many) can possibly carry the same weight as the absolute assurance of death. Leaders gave eloquent speeches. But this was only an illusion. "Under the nuclear umbrella, peace and order," thought some, while others promised, "Below the concrete, beaches." In fact, our nuclear arms *were* our peace. Without them, we have to start all over again. Where do we begin?

The End of Sovereignties, the Beginning of Peace?

Since the beginning of time, there has been nothing in history beyond the changing ambitions of sovereign powers. Only their agreements pushed war to the margins of their ordered world—into other people's territories. Can it ever be otherwise? Can there ever be a basis for peace that is not merely the temporary cessation of war? The old world order was never more than a system of agreements among the warmaking powers. Can it now become truly political? For politics is not primarily the science of power. It has been reduced to that because peace has proved impossible to guarantee, because if we wanted peace we were obliged to prepare for war. But underneath it all, politics is the art of living together. That is why politics is the only issue that matters.

Can peace be guaranteed? This question is less ridiculous than it used to be, because for the first time State sovereignty is no longer absolute. On the one hand the institution of sovereignty has been consecrated by the multiplication of the number of countries in the world, which has doubled in the past two generations. On the other hand, it is rapidly eroding. General collective principles are progressively overriding the specific national sovereignties of individual States. The order once created by the conventions of a few sovereign States seems to be taking a back seat to rules approved by *all* States—that is, to international law. This international law does not derive from the powers of the States individually; rather, it has become a common law that all States have agreed to support, financially as well as politically. This "law without a country"[67]* is today evolving into a sort of civil society of States. And this evolution could go on forever.

As time goes on, the national authority of States is being increasingly limited by supranational rules in almost every sphere of activity. These can regulate simple day-to-day matters such as the compatibility of telecommunications from country to country or they can recognize common overriding interests such as the protec-

---

*Superscript numbers refer to works listed in the numbered Bibliography at the end of this book. Asterisks and similar symbols refer to footnotes at the bottom of these pages.

tion of the ozone layer or the conservation of endangered species; they can also require our acceptance of truly political principles, such as national laws on human rights. In either case, the result is the same: the erosion of the concept of State sovereignty as such. Wealth has had a lot to do with this, as the imperatives of commerce and economics supersede those of State protectionism. Today, if a State refuses to adjust its rules to those of international commerce it quickly finds itself left behind and ignored.

Can We Put an End to War Through International Law and Economics?

For the first time in history, the world is clearly organizing itself without regard for the will of a handful of major powers. Economics and international law appear to be creating groupings on a continental scale. Both economics and politics are ignoring national borders, and countries seem to be slowly melting together, as if diluted by the mighty forces of the world market and democracy. Because they belong to nobody in particular, and because they blur State sovereignties, can these great principles finally create a political order that is ultimately stable?

What does creating a political order mean? Simply put, it means the ability to create a true sense of actually living together. The rest is nothing but organizational detail. Without this sense of community, there is no reason for national interests to coincide over an extended period of time. In the past, States lacked this sense of an overriding communal interest, so their alliances eventually fell apart; the inevitable result was war. Today, however, there is an increasing conviction that the economic and legal integration of States, by their natures and the force of their ties, can create this commonality and so eliminate all economics and political conflicts before they grow into wars.

These hopes are vain. Political integration and political stability are not the same. The former is the result of organization and common interest; the latter arises from deep personal conviction and emotions. That is why organizations and crises often develop together.

It is true that economic forces have enormous power. There is no country in the world still strong enough to oppose the international financial markets for any length of time, and only a few can even stand up to the large multinational corporations. Most States today, in fact, try to take advantage of these forces by lowering trade barriers whenever possible to facilitate the creation and circulation of wealth. Customs unions, free-trade zones and common markets are flourishing around the world. In spite of this, there is not a single part of the world where the creation of wealth or its promise have made it easier for peoples to live side by side or where they have created a willingness to do so. Southeast Asia's phenomenally increasing wealth has not brought its countries closer together—not by a long shot. The threat of poverty did nothing to stop the Slovaks from divorcing the Czechs. In such situations necessity doesn't lead to sweet reason, nor does sweet reason bring peoples together.

Is it just a matter of time? Perhaps. The future belongs to the optimists, but it is also a bottomless reservoir of utopian fantasies. Can we reasonably hope that, until we see worldwide prosperity, adherence to common international laws will be enough to create the beginnings of a truly global political order? This makes a certain amount of sense. Legal principles are the reflection of shared convictions. The law is practical and flexible; it can serve to resolve conflicts in the short term and can be a force toward nuts-and-bolts progress. Yet its whole history teaches us that such changes are slow to take shape. But it is the nature of illusions to look like reality; otherwise they are only mirages. And illusions are that much harder to fight when they concern the future. "Illusion is exaggerated faith," Balzac liked to say. Such is our faith in Law. But this utopian faith is bound to be disappointed in the end, because it misunderstands the real causes and nature of war.

Wars can follow either of two possible logical sequences, or paths. The sequence that starts with power and the threat of force, and which leads to conflicts of sovereignty, is one such; the other is the sequence of conflicts of ideas or meanings, which lead to wars of legitimacy. The former are traditional wars of ambition and conquest. They reflect the desire of a State to acquire for itself, in whole or in part, the attributes of the sovereignty of another State: population, territory, wealth, etc. The Gulf War over Kuwait is a recent example. The latter reflect, and result from, certain populations finding it impossible to live together or under an authority that they perceive as inimical. The Indo-Pakistani war over Kashmir and the war in Bosnia are present-day examples.

The system of international law is founded and premised on the existence of sovereign States. These have agreed, and continue to agree, to submit voluntarily to rules—international law—that they have defined, and continue to define, in concert. The purpose of this system is to resolve conflicts between these sovereign entities in an orderly way. This makes sense, because it is just such conflicts that for centuries past have led to wars. But today the river of history has forked. From now on, the conflicts that will develop will be those of legitimacy, not of sovereignty. For the citizens of an increasing number of countries, the State no longer symbolizes their society. The natural assumption that the State and the society are one is getting lost.

Wars today are caused not by the strength of States but by their weakness. The primary problem of security today is not the desire for power or expansion, but rather the breakdown of States.

The system of international law is helpless to combat such crises because they place it in a bind. On the one hand, international law rests on the existence of sovereign States. On the other hand, it tries to create a system of universal laws that promote principles of democracy and human rights laws *within* States. This split between peoples and States thus forces international law to choose between them. The legal system's only recourse is to create more and smaller States. In the last thirty years, the number of countries in the world has doubled. Seventy-five percent of these new countries are smaller than Massachusetts in both population and wealth. Instead of solving the problem, international law is making things worse. The old, dissolved State was weak, but the newly created ones are even weaker. The old State was not legitimate, but its successors claim legitimacy based on an aggressive affirmation of an exclusive identity. Crises in legitimacy, left unresolved, have transformed themselves into crises of sovereignty. "It is true," Candide used to say, "that killing each other is better under a flag."

International law, in its utopian way, tries in vain to apply to these conflicts the pragmatic approach that has worked so well for it in other areas. The fact is that it—the utopian system of modern international law—fails to understand the true nature of war. War and peace are not legal processes. War is essentially political, and not just because it is the crudest example of power relations at work—that is only the lesser meaning of politics. As Sun Tzu* wrote twenty-five centuries ago, "War is the province of life and death." War is the ultimate expression of the impossibility of living together. Wars over issues of legitimacy are the most intense expression of this because they set against one another parties that were formerly as one: minorities versus majorities, natives versus immigrants, nations versus States . . .

These are the wars of the future. They cannot be resolved by economic improvements or by civil procedures. Law and economics

---

*Sun Tzu is the author of the Chinese classic *The Art of War,* written about 500 B.C. The original French uses the reformed "pinyin" spelling Sun Zi. [Translator's note]

will not be able to create new political structures because they are not capable of giving groups of people a true sense of oneness. And because such a feeling is the precondition for any evolutionary change, no new political structure will ever be able to replace the legitimacy of the State.

Before we proceed, we need to define *the State* and *the legitimacy* or *illegitimacy of the State*. The State is not the country itself, nor is it the government of the country; governments come and go but the State persists. It is the essential sovereign authority of a country, which the government embodies—sometimes well and sometimes poorly.

Very broadly, when the government embodies a State effectively we call that State *legitimate* and when it embodies it ineffectively we call that State *illegitimate*.

This effectiveness or ineffectiveness of a State's government has nothing whatever to do with the presence or absence of any of the morally desirable attributes that might be inferred from the word *legitimacy;* not orderly accession to power, not the democratic process, not human rights, not freedom of speech, assembly, the press, or religion. No—a legitimate State is one with a government that provides its citizens with basic services and that enforces a level of public order sufficient to allow them to lead productive lives rather than lives ruled by fear. And the legitimate State both fosters and regulates the national economy so as to stabilize and even increase the prosperity of its citizens. A State must be strong to be able to do these things. The people of the country sense the strength and stability of their State and therefore feel a sense of allegiance to it, whether it be democratic or repressive. By contrast, if a State cannot supply basic services to its people and cannot provide a stable economic environment for them, the people turn their backs on their State and ignore it or circumvent it. Whether it is democratic or not, such a State is illegitimate.

For example, Chile under the Pinochet regime was a legitimate

State because this regime maintained public order and supported a growing economy that improved the wealth of the majority—even though most people feared and hated the oppression. The same can be said of the present Communist regime in China or of Spain under Franco. On the other hand Argentina and Portugal until recently had regimes that were doing little for their people in terms of either basic services or economic support; the people accordingly felt alienated from those States; those States were illegitimate even if not terribly repressive, at least in comparison to some others.

Only legitimate States can truly offer a future to the constituencies they represent. The breakdown of States benefits one cause only: that of war.

CHAPTER 2

The End of the Madness

What is all this about limited strikes? Why limit yourself?
Why do you want to save their lives so badly?
The whole idea is to kill the bastards. If, when all is said and
done, all that's left is one Russian and two Americans,
then we'll have won.

—General Thomas S. Power of the U.S. Strategic Air Command to
U.S. Secretary of Defense Robert McNamara

Chronicle of Death Foretold

The first nuclear disarmament treaty was signed in 1987. Nobody
foresaw it, but this treaty ended more than the Cold War; it ended
the nuclear order itself. On the one hand States, now free of the
nuclear threat, are beginning to cooperate in a thousand ways and
to grow closer to one another. On the other hand, political crises
are erupting all over the world with alarming frequency. We feel
besieged by the rising tide of disorder and by the barbarians knocking on the gates of our empire. The fall of the Berlin Wall seems to
have buried the Cold War only to bring back hot wars. What did
our planet have then that it doesn't have now?

Death. The old order belonged exclusively to death. The logic of
certain death for everyone was the only truly universal order that
the human race has ever found. As we look back at the nuclear
madness of yesterday, we are also discovering what extreme measures were needed to impose this unique order. In the collective

awareness, the views of General Power and his military colleagues carried more weight than any political wisdom or cleverness; most people were convinced that the entire world would soon disappear in a nuclear catastrophe. Auschwitz had proved that there were no limits to the horrors that humanity was capable of inflicting upon itself. Hiroshima confirmed that we possessed the nuclear capability to make the whole world walk the last mile to its annihilation.

In 1948 William Faulkner wrote, "The only question is knowing when I'm going to be annihilated." Faulkner's anxiety was that of a doomed man, both repelled and fascinated by the abyss that gaped at his feet. When questioned about the probable length of the nuclear race, Henry Kissinger answered simply, "We've embarked on a process that has no end." Was Kissinger a pessimist, or was he just drawing an inescapable conclusion? His view was shared by the general public; few thought the end would come tomorrow but most seemed convinced that nuclear Armageddon was near. In 1963, two out of three Americans believed that they would die in a nuclear war. In 1982, although the world had radically changed and was being rocked by a severe economic crisis, nuclear war remained the overriding anxiety of one citizen out of two in France, as in Italy and in the United States.[44]

We spent fifty years in a strange ongoing debate between the ideas of certain death and probable death. Even scientists fell prey to this collective folly, last seen perhaps during the Dark Ages, when many people thought the End was near. In the tenth century, as the year A.D. 1000 approached, magicians and alchemists claimed to have mathematically pinpointed the End of the World, down to the precise day and hour. A thousand years later, in the midst of the triumph of technology, the prophets of doom reappeared. This time around, computers and mathematical models replaced magical incantations and alembics, but the predictions were the same. Respected scholars such as C. P. Snow, professor of physics at England's Cambridge University, went so far as to place the mathematical probability of nuclear war at 100 percent.

Death was knocking at the door and no one could get it to go away. The world was now the disciple of Clausewitz, who wrote that "[B]ecause of their consequences, events that are merely possible should be judged as real."[110] The very people who saw no reason for war to break out were afraid that it would, thinking that an accident—always possible—would suffice, even though history offers no examples of an accidental war.[81] The man in the street, moreover, understood very little about nuclear strategy. His views on the matter were simple and deadly: "I live, or else you die."

As a result, most people were resigned to this slow march toward nuclear death. Both the American and the French voters insisted that their governments retain the option of a first strike. They also insisted on unlimited stockpiling of nuclear warheads for a response should their country fall victim to a first-strike attack.[106] West Germany followed suit, although it possessed no nuclear arms and would be the first country targeted for slaughter. As late as 1986, West Germany refused to allow the United States to promise not to launch a first strike, fearing that the enemy would thus be able to mathematically calculate the risk to itself of an attack. And so the spiral of nuclear irrationality kept tightening, as each side assured the other of its destruction, in a morbidly repeated bit of agitprop. In the end, the actual credibility of these threats was of little importance. As British Defense Minister Malcolm Rifkin explained, "It's enough that the Soviets think there's one chance in ten."

The fundamental dilemma was thus not the traditional choices of war and peace, victory and defeat. All that remained was the interminable twilight of waiting for the End. People became haunted by the uncertainty of still being here tomorrow rather than by the certainty of dying today. This was the essence of the nuclear madness: only the threat of immediate death held back global death, but the two inevitably became one in people's minds.

Because of this, nobody thought of nuclear war as *war*, to the amazement of some advocates for peace. One of these noted disapprovingly, "In London in 1981 three hundred thousand people demonstrated against the deployment of Pershing missiles, but in 1982 only three thousand demonstrated against the Falkland Islands war."[74] "Public opinion seems apathetic about real wars that tear up the planet but it is polarized about the abstract threat of nuclear war," observed another with surprise.[37] Real wars are major events with a rich past and an immense future. But there is no actual *nuclear war,* because after a nuclear strike and response there are no vanquished, no conquerors, no tomorrow. In 1986, 83 percent of Europeans were convinced that the first use of nuclear arms would also be the last. Robert McNamara admitted as much twenty years earlier when he left his post as head of the U.S. Department of Defense, where he had helped to develop the first doctrine of atomic war. In his farewell speech in San Francisco he said, "Nuclear war means this, plain and simple: the suicide, not just of armies, but of entire societies."[12] A little later, Henry Kissinger, who made his career by advocating "limited" nuclear warfare, agreed after a few years at the White House: "Limited nuclear war is a pipe dream. Nuclear war can only be absolute." In the collective imagination as well, nuclear arms were unique, absolutely reductive. No experiments could be tried with them. They were the Final Solution that humanity had invented to use on itself.

Certain Death: An Unthinkable Reality

A logic as rigorous as the nuclear one entails certain simplifications: "Your certain death guarantees my survival"—end of argument. Discussions of morality have no place in this line of thinking. Before creating a physical wasteland, nuclear war had created a moral one.[35] Most leaders considered deterrence to be effective—and that was all that mattered. Because they were willing to call this tense wait for nuclear death "peace," they judged that the means was justified by its success. If deterrence failed, then there would be no one to judge it anyway, so that wasn't worth even thinking about.

The silence of the Roman Catholic Church illustrates the complete absence of critical thinking about this issue. For the first time in two thousand years, the Church failed to incorporate a major historical event into its teachings. Over the centuries the Church had managed to incorporate pagan rituals, to interpret plagues and natural disasters, and to legitimize powers. Yet the assumptions behind certain nuclear death left it wordless. At the beginning of the 1980s, bishops in many countries tried to launch a public discussion of the morality of nuclear weapons. The attempt was disastrous. The debates created a political crisis throughout the Church. Certain bishops, notably in the United States, demanded rigorous moral consistency, even if this led to a wholesale condemnation of nuclear weapons by the Church. Others pointed out that such a stance was simply unrealistic, a rather unusual conclusion for bishops when debating matters of doctrine. In fact, the Church usually appears indifferent to passing fashions or public opinion. But now it was confronted by a very violent internal conflict.

The American bishops disagreed publicly in the press. One bishop declared that nuclear arms were unacceptable in and of themselves. The Dutch bishops prepared to say the same. Pacifist parties, often manipulated by the Soviet Union, used this unexpected support to their advantage and brought the Church to the brink of political disaster. The Vatican deeply disapproved of the ensuing debate. John Paul II, a firm advocate of *Realpolitik,* brought matters to a head when he stated his view before the United Nations: "In the present situation, deterrence, used to achieve a balance and not as an end in itself, can still be judged morally acceptable." The Pope thus avoided two possible dangers: the strengthening of the pacifist movement in Europe, and the erosion from below of the power of the Curia, which took advantage of his pronouncement to prohibit the development of doctrines at conferences of bishops. The moral leadership of the Head of the Church in the West, as well as his ability to respond to crises of power, made this papal defeat of the bishops particularly significant. Confronted for the first time by an Apocalypse not its own, the Church was unable to scale the slippery wall erected by the logic of the nuclear threat.

Nuclear deterrence thus remained a law unto itself. It had created a hermetically sealed world in which all of humanity was trapped. This trap may very well be what kept the Church unable to embrace deterrence as a viable option. In fact, deterrence is a game for men, actually for *one* man. No ancient drama or mythology was ever mad enough to imagine a situation like nuclear war, where the fate of the world rests on the judgment and decision of a single man. There is something unheard-of in the solitude thus created, something unprecedented in the idea of delegating the lives of an entire species to the decision of a single member of it. This was especially felt in France, where nuclear conflict was viewed—officially—only in its ultimate form. What an error to talk of a nuclear monarchy! For nuclear power is really a theocracy—one that revolves around the harrowing question "When will it happen?" and the God-like answer "You can know neither the day nor the hour." Looked at in this way, deterrence involves a collective destiny, even a collective death, decided upon by a single person. And the glue holding together this strange cohesion is the shared conviction that nuclear death can be invoked only by itself.

The Pathological Powerlessness of Governments

This common thread was a raw nerve in the body politic. The slightest twitch produced near hysteria. In 1973, during the Yom Kippur War, both American and Soviet forces were put on red alert. The public felt that its destiny was about to be played out on the Golan Heights, without its opinion ever having been asked or any polls taken. One can only imagine the public's reaction had it known that this decision was taken by Henry Kissinger and a few of Nixon's other advisors, as the president himself was apparently too drunk at the time to be of any use.[97] Similarly, when in 1978 a

German minister explained that the neutron bomb's ability to kill people without damaging inanimate objects made its use very likely, he transformed a technical question into a dangerous and permanent political reality. The same thing happened when President Reagan announced in 1981 that he was postponing any disarmament negotiations to an unspecified future date: Europeans and Americans alike interpreted this as a return to the coldest of Cold Wars, with an inevitable nuclear ending.

A few years later, after our amazing pullback from the abyss, the violence of these reactions seems as childish to us as the tenth century's fear of the Apocalypse. Had the American bishops been wrong after all? Had not the mere existence of such deadly nuclear arsenals been enough to assure deterrence? Why the overwhelming public anxiety? The official French position seems to have carried the day.

To think this way, however, is to misinterpret the power of the nuclear folly. All the leaders were affected, even those of the two Great Powers. Faced with certain death, they scrambled to find new theories so as to develop new options. This need to envisage alternatives was felt by both the military and the politicians. For the former, to admit that death was a sure thing was tantamount to signing their own unemployment checks. For the latter, such an admission left them no room for action. Yet nothing made any difference. For all involved, the glass wall of the logic of certain death remained impossible to climb.

Successive American leaders all found this out. Each took office believing that he could use this terrible power to gain political or diplomatic leverage. Each would be forced to admit his powerlessness in an area that seemed to leave no room to act. Every new theory met the same fate. If one theory promoted the idea of limited strategic warfare, it was accused of turning on the Allies, and turning Europe into a battlefield. If another theory tried to delay the use of nuclear weapons, it was accused of wimpiness and of leaving the Europeans at the mercy of the Soviets. The idea that only the certainty of death was postponing immediate death was deeply rooted in the minds of even the deepest thinkers.

This powerlessness could have just examined itself and noted that it was obviously caught in the trap of certain death. This is essentially what the French did: after they accepted this logic as the strongest and most unbeatable strategic position they never openly wavered from it. The 1972 *White Paper on National Defense* has the firm precision of a notarized document. By adopting this reasonable policy, however, the French deliberately withdrew from exercising any real power in world affairs. For the two Superpowers, such a renunciation was unthinkable. They would never have agreed to limit themselves to minor skirmishes so long as each was living in constant fear that the other would push the nuclear button.

This internal pairing of the logics of death and force was the very fabric of nuclear folly. If strategy could not solve the problem, then technology would. Technology had created the Weapon, so it would also find a way to make it both useful and victorious. Even the most lucid leaders gave in to this tempting line of thinking.

In 1958, an aging President Eisenhower realized that the nuclear standoff was as far as the military could go. America's dropping the bomb on Japan had not stopped the Soviets from developing their own; after that it was too late. What was needed now instead was to prevent escalation—to limit Soviet progress and decrease the chances of war. Eisenhower therefore proposed to the Soviets a moratorium on nuclear testing coupled with discussions on limiting it. But in 1959 he secretly authorized the United States to start a series of tests so small as to be undetectable. In three years over forty firings took place. In 1967, Robert McNamara conceded that the two Great Powers had equal destructive capabilities and that this would force a stalemate because "neither we nor they have the power to disarm the opponent with a first strike." And yet he could not help ending his speech by celebrating the superiority of the United States—not because of its wealth or its democratic institutions, but because of its technology. "We have nuclear superiority over the Soviet Union because we have more warheads. From now on, that's what will count the most."

This conspiracy of the logics of death and victory eroded even the most moderate thinking. Everyday citizens could not follow the many secret debates and coded pronouncements, but they could tell that the abyss was growing deeper. Few of them knew, however, just how fragile was the thread or how extreme was the insanity of nuclear weapons policy left to run its course.

The truth was slowly coming to light: not only were those in charge caught up in the same crazy spiral as everyone else, but they had lost almost all control over it. All the subtle strategic arguments and political concepts had no connection with the reality of the nuclear arsenals.

Even as politicians celebrated the liturgy of death contained, the military were developing new ways of assuring annihilation. Even today, it is difficult to imagine just how far this process had spun out of control. It is simply astounding that for forty years, in both the most powerful totalitarian State and the most advanced parliamentary democracy, politicians had virtually lost control over both nuclear proliferation and the theoretical basis for using it. Is this an exaggeration? No; see and hear for yourselves what nuclear democracy really was.

Journey to the Center of Insanity

As early as 1946, President Truman's army chief of staff asked for authorization to exert technical control over America's nuclear arsenal in order to gain more operational flexibility. Welcome to the land of political doublespeak! "Technical control" really meant full-scale appropriation of the arsenals. "Operational flexibility" meant the unrestricted right to decide when and where to use nuclear weapons in the event of war. Truman refused. In 1948, when the Soviets were blockading Berlin, the chief of staff again pushed his agenda, this time with the support of the secretary of defense, who uttered the following classic statement: "It's not prudent to entrust nuclear weapons to anyone but those responsible for their use." In one fell swoop he proved not only his limited knowledge of constitutional law, but also that the military were thinking in terms of war, were preparing for war, and had no confidence whatsoever in the resolve of the civilian authorities to allow war. Truman again turned them down in spite of pressure from his personal advisors, who were already convinced of an imminent confrontation with the Soviet Union. In 1950, the chief of staff took up his campaign again, but this time with more finesse. There was no more talk of nuclear control. The Army instead proposed taking responsibility for the entire nonnuclear arsenal in order to facilitate early deployment on the European continent. The logic of war was winning out. This time Truman gave in. He gave in again in 1951 when the military asked for control over a few nuclear weapons, citing distance as a key factor: "There's no point in having conventional weapons if, in an emergency situation, we don't have time to bring out the others." In 1952, an ailing and discouraged Truman ceded the entire nuclear arsenal to the Army and gave its chief of staff authority to define how much of it was needed. A crisis was brewing.

Over the next thirty-five years, both in the West and behind the Iron Curtain, the military were to acquire more and more power to wage total nuclear war from civilians, who were baffled by a constant barrage of lies and were systematically kept from knowing the military's true ambitions. In the United States as in France, the civil authorities tried to slow down the full-speed development of nuclear weaponry. Truman was convinced that nuclear weapons could not be used in a war against the USSR. He even wanted all nuclear weapons to be turned over to an international organization that would be under the United Nations.

At first, the world's nuclear arsenal grew very slowly. At the end of 1945, the United States had two bombs in its possession. By 1946, it had nine, by 1947 thirteen, and by the summer of 1948 a total of fifty. None of these were armed; this process took ten people over a week to accomplish and there existed only thirty or so bombers equipped to carry them. As a result, only thirty targets had been identified in the Soviet Union. Such an arsenal was great for demonstration purposes, but it would never do in time of war.

Once the military on both sides had become autonomous, things began to change dramatically. The American arsenal leaped in size to 300 bombs by 1950 and over 1,000 by 1953. Their average strength had increased a staggering ten times since Hiroshima. Concurrently international tensions were increasing, notably with the start of the Korean War. This influenced the American president to endorse the Pentagon's suggestion that a "massive strike" be the major objective of nuclear policy. By cleverly refusing to quantify "massive strike" power, the military was able to increase the size of the nuclear arsenal without answering to anyone. The official American line, which remained unchanged until 1987, was that it was necessary to guarantee the destruction of fully half of Soviet "capabilities." This vague term "capability" could be interpreted as including the armed forces, or industrial production, or the Soviet population, or preferably all three combined. This entailed striking 300 targets in 1956 but 2,000 of them by 1959. Apparently, the Soviet Union was developing faster in the eyes of the U.S. military than in those of its own Gosplan economists!

The true nature of the Pentagon's destructive autism began to come to light at the beginning of the 1960s. In 1957, the Soviets had launched the first space satellite, *Sputnik,* showing that it was able to build long-range missiles. This development of long-range rockets proved to the American military that the USSR had both the capability and the desire to use these unstoppable weapons on the United States. In 1959, the Pentagon announced that the Soviet arsenal would reach five hundred missiles by 1961, when the United States would have only seventy. In 1961, the CIA repeated this prediction for 1962. In 1962 the U.S. chief of naval operations predicted that the Soviets would reach this mark in 1963, while future German chancellor Helmut Schmidt predicted they would reach it in 1964. In actuality, the Soviets attained it in 1968. In actual fact, the Pentagon possessed accurate estimates as early as 1960: its first spy satellites revealed that the total Soviet arsenal in 1961 numbered . . . exactly twelve missiles—a number confirmed by a leading Soviet spy "turned" by the United States. This information was systematically covered up, and in its place a succession of alarmist warnings were published about the threat of Soviet nuclear-missile development.

Beginning in 1961, the Pentagon increased its list of Soviet targets to 3,500 and requested 1,000 long-range missiles. General Curtis LeMay, the founder and commander of the Strategic Air Command (SAC), explained that such a large increase was necessary "in order to facilitate the preventive destruction of deadly Soviet missiles." In so doing, he was admitting to the Senate that the Pentagon was preparing for a total nuclear war, a war that would be initiated by the United States. When the chairman of the Armed Services Committee pointed out that this contradicted official government policy, LeMay countered: "I don't know if it's the government's policy or not, but it certainly is mine." The folly surrounding nuclear war had already reached such a level that no one argued with him. LeMay's convictions in this matter were so unshakable that he took plans for a first-strike attack directly to President Kennedy in 1961. The plan guaranteed the destruction of the entire Soviet Union at the price to the United States of ten million people, "at most." The plan was discarded; LeMay was re-tained. Undoubtedly thinking that his plan had simply not seemed secure enough, in 1962 LeMay requested no less than 10,000 long-range missiles in order to guarantee the destruction of the USSR. There were now 8,000 Soviet targets.

This careening out of control did not, unfortunately, take place in the United States alone. Since Stalin's death, the Soviet military had also fought tooth and nail for control of their country's nuclear weaponry. Nikita Khrushchev was anxious to uphold his reputa-tion as a tough leader. While he retained for himself the authority to actually initiate war, by as early as 1956 he had delegated almost all war-making authority to the military. From then on, the Soviet military also sought to build on their power base. The Soviets were driven, just like their American counterparts, by the overwhelming fear that they were lagging behind in the nuclear race. Both Khrushchev and Kennedy realized that they were trapped in this infernal machine. During one of their last meetings, Kennedy asked Khrushchev, "How's it going in the USSR with the military? I can't seem to get on top of their demands." "I'm having the same problem," answered Khrushchev. "They come to see me and ex-plain that you have a dangerous lead on us and that their new pro-grams are essential. . . ."

The U.S. government was not indifferent to these develop-ments. In 1962, McNamara started a violent feud with the Joint Chiefs of Staff when he tried to impose stricter controls on their activities. He favored circulating the secret reports of their accom-plices so as to expose the lies that formed the basis of their bud-getary requests. In 1963, a report by Paul Nitze, the number three man at the Pentagon, proved that for the Soviets to be indeed as powerful as the American military claimed, they needed a budget eight times larger than that of the United States. The following year, a report by Cyrus Vance demonstrated that the capabilities attributed to the USSR by the Pentagon would require four times as many troops as the Pentagon believed they had.

Robert McNamara tried above all to control the intractable General LeMay and bring his nuclear strike theory into line with the policy of his government. McNamara wanted provisions made for limited strategic strikes as an alternative to all-out war so as to allow for progressive escalation or even a warning shot. But he was wasting his breath: years later, LeMay divulged that the "limited strike" planned against Cuba had included several hundred nuclear warheads. In 1967, on the eve of his resignation, McNamara was told by one of his colleagues that the strike plans had not been amended. He had given up trying to modify them. "I should, but I just can't afford that political battle." LeMay was immune to criticism by politicians because Congress was trapped in the no-exit game of nuclear destruction. For the American government to resign itself to the status quo meant a humiliating surrender, the failure of an America incapable, in the end, of doing any better than the Communists. This was unacceptable, but so was the persistent threat of nuclear destruction. The only answer was to find a way to wage a total nuclear war and win it.

And that dreadful pair, fear and death, continued on down their road. When Henry Kissinger came to the White House with Richard Nixon in 1968, he was a strong advocate of limited wars. He had no illusions about the consequences for America of a nuclear strike against the Soviet Union. He was stupefied to learn that the list of Soviet targets had increased from 2,000 in 1959 to 8,000 in 1962 to 25,000 in 1968. He also discovered that the Pentagon's minimum strike force comprised 2,500 warheads. Believing he had the authority, he set out to reconcile government strategy and military planning. In vain. In 1969, the chief of staff of the Air Force testified before Congress that the new multiple-head missiles would finally enable the United States to launch a first strike that would disarm the Soviet Union. In 1970, the commander of the SAC publicly repeated this statement, although it contradicted the policy announced by the president on the issue. In 1974, when a serious crisis threatened in Iran, Kissinger asked for an estimate for limited strikes on economic assets in the south of the USSR, and was quoted a figure of 200 nuclear warheads! When Kissinger left the Cabinet in 1976 there were officially 35,000 Soviet targets listed.

The Carter administration did not fare any better, but it did begin to investigate the extent of the delirium. Jimmy Carter was the only American president since 1948 to demand two things: a detailed report on nuclear strike plans and a computer simulation of a nuclear crisis in progress by way of a test case. What happened next was such a shock that it marks the beginning of the true return of authority to civilians. Jimmy Carter discovered three things.

First, he found out that the strike plans—which gave the president less than twenty minutes to make the decision to green-light nuclear war—were incomprehensible. The plans were over seventy pages long and contained dozens of options and suboptions. The only clear option was to let everything loose—which implied annihilating noncombatant countries. The second thing Carter discovered was that there was still no provision for a warning strike. The third discovery was the most revealing of all.

In the case of nuclear war, it was highly possible that the president, due to communications failures, would be completely cut off from the military chain of command, leaving them in sole control of the nuclear arsenal. This fact was brought to light by William Perry, then the number-three man in the Pentagon, who would later become secretary of defense under Bill Clinton. Perry requested a detailed review of the Pentagon's procedures to ensure that the president's orders would be transmitted without error or delay under any conditions. In fact, a report issued in 1962 by an independent organization had stated that the chain of command would not remain intact after the first fifteen minutes of a nuclear war and that as few as twenty bombs would paralyze it completely. The president would thus be forced to go to the most extreme responses at once, because he would be unable to transmit any further orders.[22] He could not, in any case, make a graduated response spaced out over time. This was blamed on negligence and on ignorance due to the novelty of nuclear conflict. William Perry's analysis begun in 1977 categorically disproved these excuses. But as late as 1979, the situation remained the same: fifty bombs would completely sever communications between the government and the military. The simulation that was run by and for Jimmy Carter gave overwhelming proof of that fact.

The Soviets, meanwhile, did not relax their efforts. Western intelligence sources learned that no fewer than 400 nuclear warheads were aimed at the fifty main American military or civilian communications and control centers. Most of these were completely ordinary structures with no special safeguards against nuclear attack: the Pentagon had in fact seen to this itself.

The Pentagon was so determined to make only total war that it had quite simply deprived the president of the means to wage war in any other way.[104] In 1978, the U.S. General Accounting Office discovered that the central surveillance system—NORAD, which gathers and interprets all radar and satellite information in order to detect possible missile attacks—had no independent source of electrical power! This may have been an oversight originally, but in 1984 the General Accounting Office confirmed that they still had not acquired one. In the meantime, it dug up a 1970 report which found NORAD's computer system to be inadequate—incapable of processing the information overload that would occur should thousands of enemy missiles and planes descend into American air space. In 1980, still no improvements had been made. An official told the GAO, "The system is incapable of dealing with a major incoming strike. It could not trace all the trajectories needed to predict which would land on American territory, nor even keep track of all the enemy missiles. Here and there, it would miss some . . ."[71] Thus the entire system was rigged for total war. At the first sign of a serious aggression against the United States, there was no other option available, given the system's limited operational capabilities and major weakness. The strategy of General LeMay had defeated that of the U.S. government after all.

The Nuclear Order: from Common Intelligence to Common Folly

The situation in the USSR was no better. In the United States, as in France, the arsenal is normally kept under a strict lockdown. A rigorous and complex protocol must be followed in order to activate it, one that rules out error, chance, and accident. Even the most vocal critics of the American system have often recognized this. The opposite long prevailed in the USSR: the nuclear launch device was permanently readied and received at regular intervals an order *not* to fire. For anyone who has experienced Soviet communications at first hand, it becomes difficult not to believe in Divine Providence . . .

Nuclear deterrence was no longer a collective strategic response to a threat; now it was a collective folly. For an increasing number of people in the military, this delirium was becoming intolerable. Nevertheless, under the Reagan administration the military's might reached unprecedented heights. Recent political events aided this apotheosis: Jimmy Carter had been discredited by his failure in Iran, while the Soviet invasion of Afghanistan confirmed the worst fears about their military expansionism—as did the new missiles which the Soviets had deployed. Ultra-precise and powerful, they possessed the first-strike capability to destroy the American missile arsenal, leaving the president only the unenviable choice of surrender or suicide. It was therefore necessary to fund an even stronger first-strike capability in the United States. Thirty years after this argument had first set in motion an insanely spiraling quest for nuclear superiority, this same fantastical logic was now pursued with renewed vigor.

In 1981, the chiefs of staff requested and obtained an increase in their arsenals—which then amounted to 8,000 nuclear warheads—of 5,000 more, to be used solely for the eradication of Soviet nuclear silos. The remainder would be devoted to obliterating the USSR and its allies from the face of the earth, thanks to a list of targets that numbered 50,000 by 1987. Annihilation was certain under any scenario; in 1987 the Pentagon asserted that even after taking a Soviet first strike, it could guarantee the destruction of 3,100 military targets and 2,300 civilian targets inside the Soviet Union . . .

In forty years, the number of targets necessary to destroy the USSR had been multiplied by 2,000. The number had doubled every four years and the guaranteed minimum now exceeded 5,000. But there is more. As long ago as 1957 Henry Kissinger, then strictly an academic theoretician, noted that the logic of total nuclear war between the two Superpowers compelled them to destroy their neighbors as well, so as to prevent strong third parties from taking advantage of the post-strike weakness of either or both. This predicted strategy soon became a real one. When in 1979 Jimmy Carter and his Polish-American national security advisor Zbigniew Brzezinski revised America's first-strike plans, they came up with something called an "accessory strike"—could anyone make this up?—which consisted of firing 300 nuclear warheads at Poland—modern warheads, each with five or six times the power of the Hiroshima bomb. It is difficult to imagine any justification for raining down a thousand Hiroshimas on a country like Poland. It is even more difficult to imagine what would be left of the country afterward.

Similar levels of attack, however, seemed to be in the works for most other sizable third parties, whether they were developed countries or not. In this real-life context, anxiety over mutually assured death suddenly seems less irrational. . . . We should think for a moment—What purpose can such a deluge possibly serve? How could anyone arrive at such inflated numbers?

The answer to the first question is simply that it serves no purpose at all. An attack of such magnitude is not only disproportionate but superfluous. For the past ten years, climatologists in the United States, Canada, and Russia have issued reports showing that a nuclear war would in all probability create a major climatic catastrophe.[70] The nuclear smoke and dust rising from burnt-out cities and industrial bases could darken the skies for such long periods of time as to cause a general lowering of temperature so great that it would freeze the oceans surrounding Europe; Africa would become as cold as Scotland and the climate of the southern continents would be like present-day Siberia's. The combination of cold, darkness, and massive ultraviolet radiation created by the destruction of the ozone layer would destroy most of the earth's vegetation. As the joint report of the three climatologists concluded, "The living would envy the dead."

The answer to the second question offers a terrifying glimpse into the minds of those involved in creating this nuclear terror. Like all modern industrial societies, the Soviet Union is a highly urbanized society (70 percent) and its main economic centers are highly concentrated. The targets reached such high numbers because each was targeted separately and no account was taken of secondary damage. Take a large industrial city like Rouen in France, for example. Two nuclear warheads of 300 metric kilotons each, or fifteen times Hiroshima, dropped at a good distance from one another, would completely devastate it. This destruction would result not only from direct damage but from secondary effects as well: gigantic fires that would destroy the huge petrochemical plants as well as the offices and industrial buildings and the docks on the Seine River. Radioactive fallout would cripple the entire region, which would be quite unable to provide care for the sick and wounded.

The American nuclear planners didn't see things that way. To begin with, they assigned one warhead to each type of target: one for the docks, one for the car factories, one for the petrochemical installations, etc. . . . Moreover, they left secondary damage out of all their damage predictions. They kept increasing the number and strength of the warheads until they were sure that the *direct* effect of *one* explosion would annihilate the target in question. The rest, including radioactivity everywhere, was icing on the cake. General Welsch, who was director of nuclear planning in 1965, confirmed as much. "All these stories about fallout and stuff falling out of clouds are crap. If a cloud passes over your garden, just wash your vegetables. All these bureaucrats and hippies have no idea what survival is."

The folly surrounding nuclear arms was colossal. There was plenty to justify the craziest fears and the most stubborn refusals to feel reassured. Neither strategic subtleties nor moral imperatives were able to weaken the conviction that some people's death meant the death of everyone else, and that there was no other guarantee of survival.

CHAPTER 3

The Twilight of the Weapon

Identical neutrality of the abyss.

—Stéphane Mallarmé

The Unthinkable Weapon

The logic of certain death has won out. The very desire to use force has been superseded by the irreducible choice posed by nuclear weapons: to use them all out or not to use them at all. It has taken a long time for this view to become the conventional wisdom. It was the fact that the nuclear arms race reached hysterical levels in the 1980s, combined with the impression that the world was once again on the nuclear path of the 1950s—several thousand bombs later—that finally made the world leaders change their thinking. Little by little, the logic of certain death drifted out of this world. Its absolute rigidity could not tolerate any change or modification, as forty years of failed attempts have proved. But a strategic concept cannot survive without changing . . . unless the world order is organized around it. This was precisely the case during the years of folly, when a conflict between two Superpowers would have unleashed the Apocalypse. After the last spasm of the early 1980s, it became clear that Henry Kissinger's "voyage without end" was indeed coming to a close. In 1985 the end of the road was reached.

Once both the Superpowers had realized that there was no way to convert this military might into a strategic advantage, it was possible for deescalation to begin. Both sides began to dismantle their nuclear arsenals.

For the first time in forty years, political realism won out over military hardware. From then on, things moved quickly; history seemed to run back like a rewinding film. In the spring of 1986 the USSR introduced the idea of the "reasonable sufficiency" of arsenals. In 1987, the leaders of the Warsaw Pact declared that "from now on the prevention of war is the main role of nuclear weapons." In the spring of 1990, NATO announced that nuclear weapons were to be used only as a "last resort," and in October, Mikhaïl Gorbachev affirmed that the Soviet Union envisaged nuclear weapons only as a means of response. The last step was taken when, in July 1991, the Soviet foreign minister proposed, in a letter to the Secretary-General of the United Nations, "concerted adoption" by the world's nuclear powers of minimal deterrence.[15] In December 1991, NATO declared it essential "to avoid an undue dependence on nuclear weapons."

In the end, the basic idea, very simple, of the French doctrine prevailed: the concept that nuclear deterrence is "a shared understanding of the threat." In order to be able to instill such a fear, the means to carry out threat need to be credible. The rest is superfluous.

The superfluities have been eliminated by the nuclear disarmament treaties. The size of the commitments made in them demonstrates the importance of the logic of war in the arsenals of the two Superpowers. Between 1984 and 2003, the United States and Russia will reduce the number of their nuclear warheads by 75 percent and their destructive capacity by 80 percent. In spite of this, global death is still assured, and cheaply: each side will keep 3,500 nuclear warheads, equivalent to 1,000 metric megatons or 200 kilograms (440 pounds) of TNT guaranteed for every human being now alive. So no need to worry; there is still enough death to go around.

There is a general trend toward reducing nuclear arms to their bare minimum. Since the Warsaw Pact has gone the way of the

USSR, this trend seems irreversible. Henry Kissinger's remark about the "voyage without end" of nuclear deterrence could become relevant in reverse. There are no guarantees that the process of reduction will ever reach a natural balance. Quite the contrary: without the obvious imminence of war, the system of deterrence is ready to implode.

Weapons Tolerated Only if They Are Reduced?

An absolute weapon demands an absolute enemy, recognizable as such. Such a situation overcomes all objections and makes the logic of mutual assured destruction appear to be the least of the possible evils. For forty years, public opinion showed a resigned, unchanging acceptance of this logic.[19] It came less from a positive allegiance than from the conviction that there was no other choice. The stability of this opinion was remarkable. Everywhere, for all those years, nuclear weapons were considered to be a necessary evil. Neither nonviolence nor unilateral disarmament ever took hold in the public imagination. On the other hand, nuclear weapons never gave rise to a nuclear militarism; nobody longed romantically to fight a nuclear battle. Whether we look at 1965 or 1985, at Chicago or Paris, the man in the street thought of the problem in terms of possessing sufficient arms to assure deterrence. Once the inevitability of the nuclear apolocalypse evaporated, public opinion again started to protest nuclear arms—always in advance of the world leaders who were trying to reduce their role. Even those people who, in the name of the lesser of two evils, had urged modernization of the nuclear arsenal and prudence in reducing it, now insisted on a rapid reduction of the nuclear forces, because they had become useless in a world no longer committed to destroying itself.

In 1985, for the first time since 1945, the great majority of Americans (78 percent) were in favor of limiting the arsenals. In 1988, 70 percent of the British and 60 percent of the French opposed any concept of a first strike, even under the imminent threat of invasion by enemy forces. In their eyes, only a response to a nuclear attack would justify the use of nuclear arms. This does not indicate a sudden pacifism, but rather the conviction that the only threats currently out there were just ordinary power struggles. Several polls reveal the depth of this fear and the complete disappearance of the awareness of an absolute enemy. By the end of 1986, 54 percent of British felt that the two Superpowers were equally dangerous; only 18 percent feared the USSR the most, while 17 percent feared American adventurism the most. In 1987 more West Germans trusted the USSR's peace policy than trusted that of the United States—59 percent versus 54 percent. From 1988 on the majority of Europeans (57 percent) firmly believed that the denuclearization of the continent would not affect the developing politics of peace. Moreover, only 22 percent felt that keeping nuclear arms would be favorable to peace: deterrence itself was following fear into oblivion. In 1989, 51 percent of West Germans felt that it had played absolutely no role in the maintenance of peace! Even Israelis (64 percent) felt that nuclear weapons should never be used, or used only if their nation were not just defeated but on the brink of being wiped off the map. The spiraling decline of nuclear arms was under way.

The leading world powers began that process by reducing such weapons to a symbolic role as the ultimate guarantors of peace. But in losing its absolute military power, deterrence also lost its absolute moral power. That is the deep significance of the citizens of the European nuclear powers refusing to use nuclear weapons except as a response to nuclear attack. The atomic weapon, because of its excessive power, wasn't a weapon at all. And it will never be one again, because it is too terrible. The end of the certainty of nuclear death is resurrecting the debate that that certainty had silenced. In the language of currency exchange, if deterrence is becoming convertible, its rate is now floating. And as the nuclear issue becomes relative, it becomes possible to see it in moral terms. Those 500 megatons no longer represented just the weight of France's security alone but also that of hundreds of millions of corpses. And once you start counting the number of possible dead, you have to name them and thus to choose them. Once nuclear death has lost its universality and its certainty, it once again becomes intolerable.

By limiting itself, nuclear deterrence signed its death warrant. Only the nuclear apocalypse lay beyond all judgment, because there history would end. Here the uniqueness of the logic of certain death can be plainly seen. It was not only the scope of its capacity for destruction that made the nuclear order credible—it was the certainty of its fatal outcome. The depth of the spiraling madness counts for more than the depth of the abyss. The logic of nuclear deterrence ended, paradoxically, with its own success. Yesterday it promised a war of cataclysmic proportions; today it embodies a war that will never take place. The millions of potential victims are no longer the anonymous guarantors of our survival; now they are identifiable hostages of our politics. In such an atmosphere, the very logic of certain death is unsustainable and the reciprocity that used to give it credibility today is a reason to abandon it. "It's enough to just stop it."

Nothing illustrates this turnaround better than the transformation of the nuclear disarmament negotiations. From 1949 to 1986, those discussions revolved solely around the "limitation" of nuclear arsenals. In a sophisticated ritual, endless discussions confirmed the status quo, which was constantly expanding. The limitations that had been discussed between 1973 and 1979, for example, were half the size of the expansion of these arsenals during this period. Everything turned around when the logic of war was abandoned in 1986. Starting in 1987, the United States and the Soviet Union agreed to abolish all medium-range nuclear missiles based in Europe. To Europeans, these weapons of limited power (compared to others, that is) symbolized the certainty of their nuclear doom at the hands of the two Superpowers. For the Superpowers, they symbolized the conviction—renewed every so often—that a nuclear war limited to Europe was both feasible and winnable. The abolition of these weapons has left only the Superpowers' enormous strategic arsenals facing off—a way of saying that they were renouncing war. Deterrence was clearly an all-or-nothing matter.

From 1990 on, disarmament became a simple game of unilateral announcements. The nightmare of some and the goal of others for forty years, the denuclearization of Europe was accomplished with a few exchanges of letters over the last three months of 1991. Without prior warning or consultation, President Bush, on September 27, 1991, let the Allies know that the United States was withdrawing its nuclear weapons from Europe. For over forty years they had embodied trans-Atlantic unity, had been the pretext for the presence of American troops in Europe, and had caused the most violent arguments in NATO; with one stroke of a pen, these weapons vanished. There were no debates about this decision, no dissenting opinions: the very lack of reaction, even lack of interest by public opinion on both sides of the Atlantic showed better than anything else could that they had abandoned the nuclear religion.

In the same way that the decline of the Church has led to vague deism rather than militant atheism, the decline of nuclear deterrence is more of a progressive dissolution into increasing abstraction than an outright rejection. Just as nuclear weapons remained a viable option as long as their numbers increased, they will remain tolerable as long as their numbers diminish. As with the Church, the price of this tolerance is a lessened presence in the real world.

Bringing France Into Line

Inescapably, the French nuclear forces will also be called into question. For a moment it seemed as if the two Superpowers would endorse the French attitude of *juste mesure,* or "exact proportionality."

But the downward progression will show itself to be much harder to withstand than the wild upward trajectory that preceded it. France's nuclear self-sufficiency had as an immediate corrolary *not* being linked to the gesticulations of the two Superpowers, which had started their arms race early, had overarmed themselves, and had tacitly but firmly agreed to commit themselves only when it suited them both to do so. That the two Superpowers should begin to bring their nuclear arsenals down to a more rational size was a precondition that France had long set for participating in an eventual nuclear disarmament program.

France demanded before joining such a program that the disarmament be executed by the two Superpowers in all domains: nuclear, conventional, chemical, and outer space. In two years, all of these conditions became realities.* In setting these conditions, France had imagined a utopian world that would endorse its strategic concepts. But no one believed that this world would ever really exist, so no one had thought of the political consequences of the evolution of such a morally desirable development. Its first effect was to erode the specificity and the uniqueness of the French nuclear policy, a position that had been a source of French pride because it combined efficiency with wisdom. The return to common law, even French common law, was not desired by the French; for them it meant being forgotten, thus losing importance. This

---

*The disarmament treaties signed in July 1991 and June 1992 reduced nuclear arsenals by more than 75 percent. The conventional-arms-reduction treaty for Europe was signed in 1990 and the treaty on overall size reduction in June 1991. They concentrate mostly on rebalancing conventional forces in Europe, without taking into account the withdrawal of Soviet troops, the dissolution of the Warsaw Pact, and the disintegration of the USSR. An international convention signed in 1993 provides for the elimination of chemical weapons: it provides for the elimination of all chemical stockpiles and of all means of chemical weapon production, and a strict surveillance system. Finally, the Clinton administration's abandonment of the Star Wars program in May 1993 buried the last major project in the arms race in outer space—a race that henceforth would be beyond the technical and financial reach of any other power.

fear is now being justified, and it will be increasingly difficult for France to stay out of the movement toward disarmament, in which the effects of announcing it weigh more heavily than the realities.

This erosion affects not only the arsenal, but also the philosophy underlying France's nuclear policy, which is now beginning to seem dated to those who developed it. The youngest of the "Generals of the Apocalypse"* who contributed to building French nuclear policy was born in 1918. The 200 managers and experts on French nuclear policy that François Mitterrand brought together in May 1994 were notable first and foremost in that most of them were at least sixty years old—as if French nuclear policy had been the adventure of a generation without descendants. The fuzzy definitions of a country's vital interests, the insistence placed on measuring the latter in numbers of lives,[19] the choice of massive strike attacks on cities—all are elements of our nuclear policy that our view of the world has made intolerable to public opinion and to a growing number of French political leaders.

This groundswell is carrying along the deliberately foggy British nuclear strategy as well as its carefully-laid-out French counterpart. Rather than forming a precise list of conditions, the British consider disarmament to be acceptable "as long as it does not affect the quality of the deterrence." But such a criterion presupposes a benchmark, that is to say an adversary that is at least implicitly named. Without a specific enemy in mind, how can one defend the size or quality of any arsenal? The problem is openly discussed in the United Kingdom, where the government has decided to buy a fleet of nuclear submarines from the United States to replace its current twenty-year-old fleet. For the first time, the majority of

---

*Nickname given by François Géré[52] to the four generals, symbolizing the "nuclear army" and its doctrine in France: Beaufre (born 1902), Ailleret (1907), Gallois (1911), Poirier (1918).

public opinion opposes this modernization of the arsenal. At a time when the government is cutting back on public spending and scaling down its social programs, both ordinary citizens and the military resent this huge investment as a complete waste of money. How could the government possibly justify a program of arms modernization linked to a military strategy that is increasingly being rejected both by public opinion and by the military itself?

A Never-Ending Twilight?

This is indeed the end stage that we see developing. Not only is mutual assured destruction losing its credibility, but nuclear arms themselves are losing all but symbolic relevance. This is nothing but the gentle death of the entire concept. Robert McNamara stated in 1967 that "Every future age of humanity will be nuclear." Only one generation later, it is no longer that simple; nuclear weapons had already lost the basis of their role even before their glory days were over.

After forty years in the shadow of nuclear arms, it has become clear that they can only play an equalizing role if their arsenals are endlessly increased. Beyond a certain point, however, they lose all strategic significance. Nuclear weaponry is no longer either a gauge of power or, even less than it used to be, a realistic way to fight a war.

In fact, it never was one. Early on, it became apparent that the vital interests that would justify using nuclear weapons were few and would only become fewer over time: for Moscow, the invasion of a Warsaw Pact country or of the Kurile Islands; for Washington, the invasion of Europe, Japan, or the Persian Gulf, would have been unacceptable no matter what the cost. Moreover, in 1957 Henry Kissinger openly questioned whether the invasion of Europe would be sufficient cause for a nuclear entanglement: "Faced with such a risk, if it came down to sacrificing Chicago or Boston, even the defense of Europe—the cornerstone of our foreign policy—would have to be seriously debated."[10] Twenty years later, in 1979, he stated frankly that the United States could no longer afford such a risk. As for the other allies of both Superpowers, it was clear from the start that they did not warrant taking such a huge risk, no matter how important they might be considered at a particular point in time.

Every crisis that has erupted during the nuclear era has demonstrated to what lengths those in power have gone to avoid nuclear confrontations. At the end of the 1940s, the United States did not use atomic power to conserve its nuclear monopoly or to stop the Soviet takeover of Eastern Europe. At the beginning of the 1950s, the U.S. refused to use nuclear arms in Korea, in spite of having been taken by surprise and holding a strategic position that was uncertain for a long time. In 1953, President Truman opposed the nuclear bombardment of Manchurian airports and fired General Douglas MacArthur, whom he judged too pronuclear. Neither Kennedy nor any of his successors ever even considered using nuclear weapons in Vietnam.

Recently declassified records of the Cuban missile crisis show that in 1962 President Kennedy had planned to retreat and not enter into an open conflict if the Soviet Union had stood firm. At the time, the USSR possessed only twenty missiles capable of reaching America and Washington knew that. However, Kennedy never entertained the possibility of using the crisis as a pretext for destroying the USSR. On the contrary. When Khrushchev announced the withdrawal of Soviet missiles from Cuba, Kennedy had been about to propose disarming the U.S. missiles stationed closest to the USSR—in Turkey—in exchange for the withdrawal of the ones in Cuba. The Soviet Union was following a similar course. Access to Soviet military files reveals that the Soviet Union was ready to use nuclear weapons without restriction to defend its vital interests, but it never considered using them elsewhere, in Korea or in Afghanistan.

Recent wars, from the Gulf to Yugoslavia, have shown a surprising consistency in sincere-seeming pacifist tactics that underline the resounding uselessness of nuclear weapons.[1,38,39] As to future wars, the very actions of the leading world powers show that they see no use for nuclear arms: the withdrawal of most tactical weapons from Europe, the denuclearization of South Korea and the Philippines by the United States, and of Vietnam by Russia. . . .

In 1946 there were two nuclear weapons on the planet. In 1986, there were about 60,000, or the equivalent of two metric tons of explosive for each living person—and just a few grams of explosive in a land mine kills someone every single day. For forty years, the nuclear powers tried to cheat the logic of mutual assured destruction, hoping that extra weapons would provide a definitive advantage which would permit victory without the immediate destruction of the victor. But every increase in nuclear arms has only increased the probability of death for all involved. This was the unprecedented spiral of the past half-century: a certainty of death that each attempt to escape made that much more certain. For forty years, humanity—the chosen people of the pathological nuclear god—waited for the nuclear apocalypse to destroy it, but it never came. Just as the Year 1000 had a January 2nd, the Berlin Wall fell quietly; its remains were distributed to masons, sold to collectors, and replaced by tranquil avenues.

The torchbearers of nuclear arms clamor that nuclear technology will never be disinvented; this is certainly true, barring a sudden global attack of amnesia. After the death of his servant Jerôme, Immanuel Kant posted a sign over his desk that read: "Remember to forget Jerôme." The world will not make an effort to forget nuclear arms. It will just continue to go on as before.

Nuclear arms will not disappear. They will remain "inalienable and vain," in a hazy twilight between memory and warning.

CHAPTER 4

The End of the Alliances

Powerful States can do without allies and small ones should
not even hope for them.

—The Due de Lévis (1764–1830), *Maximes politiques*

Nuclear Power as an Income-Producing Asset

Nuclear arms argued against their own use so effectively that they
were disarmed. Therefore it is wrong to say that nuclear arms were
useless. This very persuasiveness is an indication of their success. It
is true that nuclear arms did not stop wars; in fact they were unable
to stop *any* war, except a nuclear one. Paradoxically, nuclear deterrence prevented the destruction of humanity as a whole, but could
do nothing to stop the death of countless people in conventional
wars. Just as Earth's magnetic field orients all compasses in the
same direction, the certainty of universal death pointed to a course
forbidden to all. "Nuclear peace" never existed: rather, nuclear war
never took place. Nuclear arms were not a guarantee of peace;
rather, their very existence produced order.

The Superpowers insisted on ascribing a meaning to every event.
The most appalling conflicts were tolerated calmly, but never with
indifference. Any little incident in international relations—any petty
conflict—could lead to a confrontation and any confrontation to a
full-blown disaster. The logic of certain nuclear death ruled the superpowers as absolutely as Fate ruled the gods of ancient Rome. The
Superpowers were coerced into getting along. From then on, their

confrontations were jointly rehearsed and their diplomacy a theatrical show. All the meetings, press conferences, signing ceremonies, and innumerable negotiation sessions were rituals performed before the altar of deterrence. They were exorcisms of nuclear death. But they were also a way of consolidating the Superpowers' joint domination of the nuclear order. It was the desire of both for hegemony— and not technical difficulties—that each time doubled the length of the arms-control negotiations: three years for the first negotiations, six for the next, and twelve for the last ones. When the two Superpowers decided to disarm, first in 1987 and then in 1991, they needed only a few weeks to agree on principles and a couple of months more to agree on how to carry out the process.

These negotiations marked the transition from confrontation, which had become impossible, to a more and more complex management of the income from nuclear power. And what an income it was! All this reverential ritual consecrated the central role of the nuclear powers in the international order. They were the only permanent members of the United Nations Security Council—and not just because they were clever. The hierarchy of nations was determined by the possession of nuclear weapons. They *were* the order of the world.

Forced Marriages

The Superpowers' control over world politics was jealously guarded. The logic of certain death compelled alignment. On both sides, the global nature of the danger bound all the countries together; the most powerful countries, with the most to lose, claimed as their due the absolute loyalty of the others. Until the mid 1960s, the nations of Europe were host to both Soviet and American nuclear weapons, yet without knowing their number, type, or location! In this respect the two Superpowers treated their respective halves of Europe virtually alike.

Unknown to the Allies, the Pentagon was rapidly increasing its store of nuclear weapons. The Europeans were growing increasingly concerned about being left completely in the dark about these matters, given the growing Soviet threat and the resulting increased risk of war. In 1962, the American government guaranteed openness within NATO; twenty-five years later, however, the ambassador of the United States to NATO from that period admitted, "We did everything we could to prevent it from happening."[79] Meanwhile in the East, the Kremlin was putting in place the means to implement its doctrine of immediate nuclear war. While the Western European countries harbored dozens of nuclear weapons, in Eastern Europe the number reached into the thousands. In 1991 and 1992, the Red Army repatriated to Russia no less than 15,000 of them.

Both the Soviets and the Americans did everything in their power to guarantee good order among their allies. Each was able to achieve this with all but one rebellious ally: China for the former and France for the latter. Since both these countries were of secondary military importance, it was unreasonable that they should aspire to play a major political role. China's increasing domestic troubles quickly reduced that country to a ferment of instability. France posed a much more difficult problem. For the United States, the French policy of deterrence was not something the French had a right to pursue but a dangerous deviation from its own nuclear policy; highly coercive methods were used to bring France back into line.

At the June 1962 Atlantic Council meeting in Athens, American Secretary of Defense Robert McNamara presented to the allies the new administration's doctrine of graduated response. It was the first attempt to escape from the all-or-nothing nature of nuclear weapons. Rather than going straight to an immediate massive strike, McNamara explained, the United States would begin with limited strikes whose strength would be incrementally increased if necessary. Negotiations would continue during the first nuclear exchanges — whose increase in power, judiciously calibrated, would quickly convince the Soviets that they could not win such a confrontation and would force them to negotiate. This presupposed, of course, that the bombings would be controlled by one person and that that one person would not lose control of his mission and launch an all-out nuclear strike. McNamara explained without mincing words that France was to stay out of these negotiations entirely and would never be permitted to carry out her own doctrine of a massive strike against Soviet cities. Off the record the Americans also made it clear that, if necessary, the United States would itself take care to prevent France from launching an all-out war against the USSR on her own.

The Franco-American conflict over the concept of limited nuclear war was important enough to result in France's withdrawal from NATO's military authority in 1966. "Graduated response may be imposed on us, but we don't have to accept it," De Gaulle declared immediately in 1962. He felt that a nuclear war could not be so precisely controlled and he was convinced that to believe otherwise would only increase the risk of provoking such a war. Unpublished documents show that he understood that the main goal of the United States was to control its European allies while avoiding the risk of exposing itself to a nuclear strike, and to keep its hands free in order to divide the world with the USSR. De Gaulle concluded that the United States would use any means at its disposal to consolidate its power and that it would tolerate no opposition. "The more nuclear power develops, the less integrated France will be in NATO," he declared in 1962. For four years, France campaigned to prevent this doctrine of flexible response, which it considered too hawkish, from becoming official NATO policy. It was nevertheless imposed by the Americans but only became official NATO doctrine in 1967, after France's withdrawal.

The United States preferred alienating one of the main NATO powers to relinquishing its monopoly over nuclear policy. Control over the latter was deemed more important than any political cooperation or "community of Atlantic values." During the 1981–1983 turmoil over the presence of missiles on the European continent, the Soviet Union—with the tacit consent of the United States—tried hard to force France to get back into line by assimilating its forces with those of the United States. The two Superpowers had effectively combined to make this dissent and unpredictability go away. The nuclear order was not only mandatory but monolithic.

Not in My Back Yard: the Real Privilege of the Nuclear World Order

Political dominance was not the ultimate goal of the masters of the nuclear order. The real privilege for them was that of waging wars solely in countries other than their own. The logic of mutual assured destruction led to a major tacit conspiracy: just as it assured the prevention of a nuclear apocalypse, it guaranteed that wars would be limited to nonnuclear countries. For thirty years, this guaranteed peace to the two Superpowers and war to everybody else. General de Gaulle immediately interpreted the American policy of flexible response in this way. He saw that, while limiting the risk of escalation, it simultaneously made nuclear war limited to Europe more likely. The very term "flexible response" was a masterpiece of ambiguity. For the Europeans, the emphasis was on a *response* linked to American policy; for the Americans *flexibility* was the key and allowed for moderation. The disagreement could not be overcome. On the one hand, the certainty of universal death created a joint destiny for the Allies that justified the nuclear order imposed by the United States. On the other hand, it made the Americans want to free themselves of this joint destiny and made the Europeans fear that the United States might succeed. The logic of certain death forced solidarity on all the parties even while it prevented them from truly embracing it. Americans and Soviets shared the desire to contain nuclear war within Europe, while the Europeans were obsessed with preventing them from doing so.

The relationship between the United States and its allies for over forty years can best be summed up as the desire of the former to avoid commitment and of the latter to force them into it. This was the fundamental conflict of nuclear diplomacy. It pitted the United States not against its Soviet enemy but against its European friends, who were forced to swear absolute fealty in the name of a commitment that was nothing of the kind.

These ambiguities weighed especially heavily on the relationship between the United States, France, and what was then still West Germany. The French and the Americans both courted the West Germans to try to win them over to their respective sides of the dispute. "The Americans are not trustworthy; what we need is a European defense system," the French proclaimed. "Do you really think that the French would defend you against the Soviet Union?" retorted the Americans. Neither side fully convinced the West Germans. They asked the French, "Will you share your nuclear weapons with us?" and the Americans, "Will you make Frankfurt as important as Boston in terms of your nuclear response?" Getting no satisfactory answers, West Germany kept its distance from both countries and pursued its own policy toward the USSR. But every crisis reawakened West Germany's concerns.

In fact, while presenting a united front to their common enemy, for thirty years the three powers held divergent views about the use of nuclear weapons in Europe. "The later the better," said the Americans, who wanted above all to avoid committing themselves. "The sooner the better," retorted the French, who were convinced of the impossibility of winning a traditional war and skeptical about the sincerity of the United States. "As soon as necessary," concluded the West Germans, who wanted solidarity without catastrophe. It was only the inevitable dimensions of any such nuclear catastrophe that imposed an integrated policy on all the players.

The End of the Alliances

This enforced cohesion can no longer be imposed: nothing will ever replace the unifying power of the threat of universal death.

The receding of the tide has not caused the disintegration of the alliances; it has only revealed rifts that were already there. Only the fear of nuclear destruction was able to prevail over such powerfully divergent political interests. No accord or alliance will ever be so powerful. The military alliances are not alone in disappearing with the end of the nuclear imperative. A whole network of deeply felt bonds that seem to have other origins and to be stable and durable are also in the process of dissolving—unless they adapt themselves. But all indications are that none of them will endure, to such an extent was the shared logic of certain death the only basis for them.

The USSR is a perfect example. It is well known that the nuclear order gave the USSR Superpower status. But it is less well understood to what an extent nuclear power also affected its internal cohesion. Not only the Warsaw Pact but the Soviet Union itself was unified by the lurking threat of nuclear war. Unlike the United States, the USSR's status as a world power was entirely linked to war. Preparing for war justified holding together the Soviet empire; trying to prevent war led to the creation with the United States of a nuclear world order. On the day when disarmament became possible, this joint nuclear order disappeared and all the bonds it had created suddenly came untied.

The first bond to unravel was the one that linked the USSR and the United States. They had only needed one another to share the income from their nuclear power. With that abandoned, they may still cooperate on certain issues, but they are no longer tightly bound to one another. Next came the ties that the U.S. and the USSR shared with the secondary nuclear powers—France, China, and England. The Soviet Union did not even demand that those countries be subjected to the disarmament process. Finally, the ties holding together the Warsaw Pact and the Soviet Union itself collapsed. In theory, Mikhail Gorbachev could have chosen another path. The same disarmament treaties negotiated by the USSR, combined with the preservation of its political system, would have been well received by the Western nuclear powers. In practical

terms, however, the only legitimate common bond holding the Soviet Union together was its memory of past wars and its readiness
for future wars, and there was no time left to come up with a new
legitimacy, even if Gorbachev had been able to find one. Nonetheless, it is the nuclear order itself that permitted the USSR to evolve
in such a way, by guaranteeing it immunity in spite of its weakness.
For the first time, an empire was able to dismantle itself without
the risk of falling prey to its adversaries. It is revealing that the only
serious disorder to come out of this event is the uncertainty still
surrounding the fate of the nuclear weapons retained by Ukraine.
That nuclear prize represents a last common interest for the Russians and the Americans; they are no longer seeking a monolithic
world order based on nuclear weapons, but they are agreed in opposing any disorder involving them.

National Security Is the
Only Security Left Standing

This shared fear of disorder is all that the Americans and the Russians have retained from the long nuclear madness. It is the only
factor limiting the process of fragmentation that has resulted from
the end of the nuclear order. For the rest, this same end has resulted
in the rapid renationalization of security policies. The logic of certain death was not only sufficient but also necessary to impose security on the world. No other regional or global institution or
common interest can do this. In the future, however, we cannot
discount the possibility that various countries may have national
interests that coincide on other than a case-by-case basis.

Eastern Europe is a perfect case study in this respect. The renationalization of security interests was immediate in the so-called "Eastern bloc" countries. The disappearance of the Soviet yoke did not
lead them to a peaceful coexistence—nor by a long shot. Rather, it
created among them an intense will to differentiate themselves,

stemming from a desire both for self-affirmation and for acceptance by the West. It also released age-old hatreds, aggravated by half a century of fermentation. For these countries, the end of the nuclear order is bewildering. It is difficult to measure and understand the extent of their anxiety while sitting in Paris or London. They know that the West associates them with the Soviet dictatorship that once oppressed them and they are aware that they are and will remain different. They are afraid that their common past will count for more in our perception of them than their individual characters. This has led to an intense insecurity and an extremely defensive expression of their identity.

More often than not, this newfound identity is a factor in their disintegration rather than their stability. Yugoslavia, of course, provides the most brutal illustration of this. In other places, feelings run just as high, even if they are expressed less violently. The Baltic States shared forty years of oppression with a remarkable solidarity that earned them general respect, and were liberated early on despite their strategic importance to Russia. Yet the three Baltic States are not planning to organize themselves into a federation in spite of the fact that individually they are economically weak and, since the dissolution of the USSR, politically insignificant. The Poles are not exactly thrilled to find themselves alone and surrounded by Germans, Russians, and Ukrainians who look very unstable to them. The Hungarians are worried about the proximity of a Serbo-Croatian battleground and about the nationalist militarism of Serbia, a country that is home to 400,000 ethnic Hungarians. Like the Bulgarians, the Slovaks feel—not without reason—completely forgotten by the world. They are realizing, a little late, that the Czechs are in fact a screen hiding and separating them from the West, and no longer even a reluctant intermediary with it. This separation, demanded by the Slovaks themselves, has effectively absolved the Czechs of any sense of obligation toward them.

Everywhere, a deep anxiety is tormenting people's spirits and darkening their vision of the future. A November 1994 poll taken

by the European Community in the old popular democracies—
Europe, Russia, and the ex-Soviet parts of Europe—indicates as
much. In only three out of thirteen countries does public opinion
see the recent changes as good: the Czech Republic, Estonia, and
Albania. In all thirteen countries, over 60 percent of those polled
felt that democracy is headed in the wrong direction. This anxiety
exists regardless of the economic success or failure of one country
or another. As a result of this, wherever elections have been held,
voters have chosen candidates whose platforms included two
planks: slowing down the rate of change, and putting national defense first. While none of these countries face any military threat,
they are overwhelmed by an insecurity that is both the cause
and the effect of the renationalization of their stakes in their own
defense.

This revival of nationalism is not the confident affirmation of a
recovered identity, but rather an anxious quest for a new identity in
which nationalism is more important than the nation. "How did
we become such strangers to each other?" asks Vaclav Havel. Less
than two generations have passed since liberty was crushed in Bu-
dapest, less than one in Prague, and only eight years separate the establishment of military dictatorship in Poland from the fall of the
Berlin Wall. What is left between these countries? In their enthusiasm over their newfound liberty, they planned to come together in
an alliance, the Visengrad Triangle. There was no talk of defense,
and hardly any of diplomacy. Rather, it was to be a celebration of
being free together. This common vision has been so weakened
that the accord has disappeared amid complete indifference. In
spite of the dramatic history that they share, the Baltic States have
gone back to their internecine quarrels, going so far as to play off of
one another in their relations with Russia. Yesterday's hardships no
longer unite the nations of Central Europe, while tomorrow's
stakes are increasingly distancing them from each other. As with
the States of the former USSR, no agreement exists between these
countries to take advantage of their past to prepare for the future.

These countries do not form any one unit or group. Rather, they comprise an ill-assorted mosaic in which each country sees its future in the West. This shared conviction is the last nail in the coffin of any possible union.

That is why these countries want so much to join NATO, an organization formed, at least indirectly, "against them." They see NATO as a visible sign of international recognition, a confirmation of their "Europeanness" as well as a stabilizing force. The idea of NATO as their defender against future Russian aggression is secondary, and anyway a fantasy, in their eyes. More importantly, these countries need to defend themselves against one another, against the crumbling disintegration that is being exacerbated by mistrust and rancor. They see NATO less as the organization that prevented war with Russia than as a political organization that prevents war between Greece and Turkey and that is tipping the latter from the unstable and underdeveloped Middle East into the European sphere.

The reverse of this logic is disuniting the countries of Western Europe. Had the USSR remained intact, even if it had withdrawn from Eastern Europe, no one doubts that this latent threat would have favored the rapid alliance of the Eastern States with NATO, not for them but for us. The disappearance of this threat to Western Europe removes, in the eyes of many of its members, any reason to link themselves to their Eastern counterparts. An Italian official laid things out rather bluntly to a Polish colleague: "The question isn't whether or not you are ready to join NATO, but whether or not we want you to."

In point of fact, the principal members of NATO are not exactly enthusiastic about its opening itself to their former enemies. In 1991, 75 percent of Germans still thought that NATO's job was to forestall and even resolve crises in Central and Eastern Europe. This percentage had decreased to 69 percent in 1992, 58 percent in 1993 and 49 percent in 1994. Since then less than 50 percent of

German public opinion has favored granting the Central European countries NATO membership.[59] The British want at all costs to avoid being dragged into conflicts that are not theirs; the Yugoslavian crisis will have confirmed them in this position, if any confirmation was needed. However, NATO's 1949 Treaty of Washington binds member States to respond together if any individual member country is attacked. Repeal of this clause, on the other hand, would mean that the treaty would offer no protection to its present members.

The French do not want NATO—have never wanted NATO—to acquire political legitimacy; it is a defensive alliance and should remain one. Furthermore, it seems counterproductive to provoke Russia by bringing NATO to its doorstep. "It would be perceived like the Ottoman troops at the gates of Vienna in the eighteenth century," noted one politician. As for the Americans, they favor political cooperation with Russia, which completely opposes extending NATO membership to certain of its neighbors. The Russian military are developing an almost claustrophobic fear of encirclement; this, together with the humiliation they feel at their loss of the Cold War, could have grave and unforeseen consequences. Furthermore, the United States would like to avoid increasing the Atlantic Alliance's Eurocentrism, which can only dilute American influence on it. The ceaseless efforts of some member States of the European Union to reinforce it is already enough of a concern to the United States, especially since Canada has withdrawn its forces from Europe.

The Inexorable Erosion of NATO

This problem may very well be solved by the dissolution of NATO itself, since this organization was also held together by the nuclear threat. With the disappearance of NATO, the political cohesiveness imposed by the Soviet menace will vanish as well. In 1991, the United States unilaterally decided to denuclearize the NATO forces, thus ending the strategic link betwen the two shores of the Atlantic. All of the minutely detailed declarations by NATO on the importance of the trans-Atlantic link and the nuclear guarantee it provided were sent into oblivion at one stroke by the signature of the president of the United States. Founded on the nuclear world order, NATO's military coherence will not survive that order's disappearance.

The real world is no longer the world of nuclear weapons. Many observers agree with Pierre Lellouche: "What destroyed the reign of the nuclear order was the fact that, beginning in the 1940s, it was systematically bypassed."[91] Apart from a few French theorists, no one ever believed that nuclear power was sufficient, as noted recently by an American strategist. "Nuclear power is not limited; therefore it is insufficient."[11] Starting in 1967, Robert McNamara emphasized the fact that "there are levels and types of aggressions that cannot be deterred by nuclear weapons alone."[84] Nuclear weapons are now seen as not only insufficient but useless; note the general indifference that greeted the denuclearization of Europe. NATO itself now attributes to nuclear weapons only a symbolic insurance value. In November 1992, a British defense minister declared: "It's not by inventing new wartime functions for nuclear weapons that we shall deter the aggressions or menaces which we shall face from now on." However without a nuclear order there exists no order at all within NATO. The British are aware that the divergent interests of its members are leading NATO down the road toward marginalization, and they also see that the secondary place now assigned to nuclear weapons means that they will play no role in creating a European union. The Italian minister of defense was recently reduced to arguing that "[M]aintaining the cohesion of the Alliance will be the main role of nuclear weapons from now on."[6]

As the grand alliances imposed by the nuclear order come apart, they leave each country to determine its individual defense needs, which, for most governments and citizens, seem modest. In the West we have witnessed no sudden rise of antimilitarism, but rather the spread of the view that no great threat exists. In losing its absolute imperative, both national security and its costs have become once again matters for negotiation.

François de Closets illustrated this perfectly when he criticized lavish arms expenditures in his recent book on waste in public spending. "The real security interests for the French today involve the Ministries of Urban Development, Health, and the Interior, rather than the Ministry of Defense."[68] French public opinion seems to agree with De Closets, being more concerned with unemployment and crime than with events in Algeria and Tadjikistan. This attitude has disastrous consequences for NATO. Having already lost the coherence imposed by adversity and nuclear weapons, NATO is now losing its military skeleton, the last stage before it is politically erased. The renationalization of defense policies has now made it possible to drastically reduce defense costs.

An Alliance Without Weapons?

In the past five years, the yearly military expenditures of the NATO countries have diminished by 20 percent, or approximately FF 600 billion* ($120 billion) *per year.* In 1994 defense expenditures by the three principal European countries were FF 85 billion ($17 billion) less than in 1988. "The peace dividend" is not just an expression. Everywhere we look, defense equipment is being reduced, if not completely dismantled. Since 1987, land-based armed forces have decreased by 25 percent in Germany, France, and England; by 35 percent in the United States; by 40 percent in Spain; and by 50 percent in Belgium and the Low Countries. Military conscription has been eliminated in Belgium and Holland. Only a portion of the remaining troops will be on active duty: one unit out of two in Spain, one out of four in Germany. Belgium has assigned over half of its remaining troops to the "Eurocorps" created by France and Germany, which weakens NATO, or so NATO claims. The figures that reveal

---

*FF = French francs [Translator's note]

the defense cutbacks most clearly concern spending on military equipment. (The overall military budget shows less change because salaries constitute so much of it.) Spending on hardware had reached a peak in 1987 in all the major countries. Since then, it has decreased by 15 percent in France, by 20 percent in the United Kingdom, by 25 percent in West Germany, and by 30 percent in the United States. Moreover, the great international programs that symbolized the Allies' joint commitment have been abandoned without much regret. The European fighter plane is dying a slow death, the modernization of NATO's aerial surveillance has been abandoned, as has the joint frigate program, a similar program for helicopters will probably soon be abandoned too. All in all, the portion of these countries' GNP allotted to defense spending has declined by an average of 20 percent in eight years. Such Draconian spending cuts have rarely been seen.

The most revealing thing is that none of these decisions has caused a ripple within NATO, in spite of their importance to it. In 1991 the United States deactivated its entire nuclear arsenal in Europe. In 1992 it cancelled its annual contribution to the budget earmarked for modernizing the infrastructures of NATO. In 1993, Canada unilaterally decided to withdraw its troops from Europe. All these examples of the indifferent renationalization of defense policies show how far national security and national defense have fallen out of favor as reasons for the political integration of States. It also displays the indifference of Europe's States to the operational future of NATO, that is, its function. In practical terms, all these national decisions add up to an erosion of NATO that greatly concerns those who continue to defend its military importance. But each new attempt to repair this erosion further confirms the extent of this general indifference to NATO. Thus, hoping to maintain some degree of unity and productivity, the British and the Americans have imposed the creation of a "Rapid Reaction Force" which would be able either to combat limited threats (yet to be found!) or to serve as front-line shock troops while awaiting reinforcements. But this first line of defense could be mistaken for the kind of stateless ragtag armies that crisscrossed Central Europe during the Thirty Years' War in the seventeenth century! A British division finds itself with a brigade of Italians and a brigade of Portuguese, while an airborne division groups together German, British, Belgian, and Dutch brigades. Yet another brings together Italian, Greek, and Turkish soldiers; in this division we may imagine that the Italians spend more time keeping the Turks and Greeks from fighting each other than all three spend in fighting a common enemy . . .

An Alliance Without a Plan

Today, NATO is struggling to expand its role beyond its original function as a "community of Atlantic values."* Not that this first definition is unimportant today: the Atlantic Alliance brings together all the main industrial countries except Japan and Australia. Manfred Woerner, the former secretary-general of NATO, led a quiet campaign to admit these two absentees. But he suddenly realized that by doing so he was completing the transformation of a once-formidable political and military institution into a mere club for rich countries. This caused him profound embarrassment. Not only did this episode reveal—almost by accident—Woerner's confusion about the Atlantic Alliance; by bringing in member States from the other side of the world, he was virtually condemning the Alliance's military organization. For that is really what is at stake. The Atlantic Alliance in itself poses no problems for anyone.

The real question is NATO—that is, the military organization that this Alliance has developed and that formed this Alliance into an almost fully integrated military entity, at least for its European members. By losing its military cohesion, NATO also loses its political cohesion. The main thrust of the 1949 Treaty of Washington has gone from Article 5 (which establishes the principle of a uni-

---

*Article 1 of the NATO statutes.

fied Allied response to an aggression against any of its members) to Article 4 (which emphasizes the nature of the Atlantic Alliance as a political forum). This has changed NATO from a community that has chosen to share its real-life destiny to a community that affirms common values only in the abstract. How will this change manifest itself in practical terms? All of the European countries are aware of NATO's metamorphosis from a pragmatic institution to a theoretical one, and aware too of its inexorable slide toward dissolution.

The current debate is no longer about *how* to organize the military aspects of NATO but *whether* there is still a reason to do that. This change of emphasis has occurred in the meetings of the NATO heads of State over the course of the past five years. In July 1990 at the London Summit no one felt confident enough to assert that the Soviet threat had disappeared, and that was a prudent conclusion. But by September 1991 at the Rome Summit the world had truly changed: the main disarmament treaties had been signed, the breakup of the USSR had been confirmed, the Red Army was in retreat, democracy had triumphed in Moscow, and the Communist Party had been outlawed there. After fifty years of struggle, NATO had "won."

It took a while for NATO to realize that the end of its enemy was also its own. As the years went by, for the tens of thousands of officers and functionaries that it employed, as well as for countries such as Holland and England that had become attached to the American presence, NATO was much more than a war machine. In their eyes, NATO embodied liberty itself. By "winning" the Cold War, NATO had established the rule of democracy; by diversifying its missions, it would reign with democracy forever. To set the future in motion, NATO's Secretary-General Manfred Woerner proposed that the organization provide aid to the poorer regions of the ex-USSR. He made this proposal in December 1991, with deep sincerity.

For Manfred Woerner this was a sublime moment in history. By making the transition from war to aid, NATO would show that it was truly the incarnation of all the humanitarian values that it had been ready to fight for in the past. In this way NATO would display both its true colors and its magnanimity. To Woerner this was obvious. The very strength of his emotion showed both the depth of his feelings on this subject and his conviction that they were shared. "His" was, thus, the most powerful and the most generous of organizations. Unfortunately, this conversion from a military organization to one that makes bulk distributions of food was criticized by several European countries. The English wanted NATO to economize before looking for new ways to spend its money. The Germans did not want NATO's aid to compete with the aid that they were already supplying to the USSR, which for them was a privileged form of political influence. The Belgians thought NATO was unqualified for the task at hand, and the French thought—rather more bluntly—that NATO was sticking its nose where it did not belong. Woerner was crushed—not so much by the rejection of his proposal as by the sudden revelation that most member States saw NATO simply as a military organization, one whose military role and operating assets were bound to diminish and which had no other natural purpose.

Since then, every major international event again raises the question of what role NATO can play in it: blockade the coast of Yugoslavia, intervene in Bosnia, jump-start international political organizations, handle the "threat of the South"*—anything will do. There is something desperate about the quest to find any role whatsoever for NATO, which has begun to resemble the search of a thirsty animal for a waterhole. If the question of NATO has

---

*In European usage, "the South" is shorthand for the less-developed countries of southern Europe and often, by extension, the whole of the less-developed world; likewise "the North" is shorthand for the more-developed countries of northern Europe and often, by extension, the whole industrialized world. That is the meaning of these terms in this book. [Translator's note]

found no answer, it is not from lack of creative suggestions but rather because the need for security is no longer an integrating factor among the sixteen countries of the Atlantic Alliance—on the contrary. It is neither French opposition nor American clumsiness that has brought NATO to a standstill. Rather, it is the lack of a consensus or even of any desire for a consensus. The noticeable softening of the French position since 1992 has not altered the uneasiness at the heart of NATO. It is precisely because the organization is crumbling that the president of France has occasionally allowed his defense minister to participate in its operations. The defense minister is permitted this participation precisely because the meetings that he attends no longer have anything to do with the military administration of the West—NATO's former business. This participation is, case by case, an indication of what NATO is becoming: a provider of services to international *political* organizations—and NATO is not itself a political organization. The United States' withdrawal from the verification of the Bosnian arms embargo in November 1994 finally opened the world's eyes to what NATO has become. It is no longer the embodiment of an alliance, but rather the principal vehicle for the domination of the United States over European defense.

Inevitably, a Parting of the Ways

In both blocs, the post Cold-War period has led to some surprising paradoxes. The lack of a sense of insecurity in Western Europe and the persistence of a sense of insecurity in Eastern Europe have led to parallel organizational breakups. Defense has once again become national in nature, not to say nationalistic. Not only is there no longer a worldwide political logic of security; there is not even a regional one. Immediately after the breakup of the USSR the members of NATO thought that they shared a common future, and the large countries of central Europe started to map out a regional organization. But some time has elapsed, and today each country follows its own path of indifference or anxiety. What does tomorrow hold in store? There is no reason to be optimistic in view of so much flight from the centers of power.

We see the same desertions among the neutral and nonaligned countries. Their only political similarity, it turns out, was their attitude to the nuclear order. As a political grouping they are disappearing along with it, for their only link was the fact that they were not formally allied to either of the blocs. What else could Switzerland, India, and Peru have in common? A large number of developing nations chose to remain nonaligned. In part this expressed their shared colonial past and a refusal to take sides in conflicts between countries whose wealth seemed (from a less-developed perspective) to link them to one another more than their political differences separated them.

What is nonalignment today? Military nonalignment no longer makes sense: Switzerland is neutral—and neutralized—more by its refusal to join the European Union than by staying out of NATO. Austria, Sweden, and even Finland are ready to abandon any nonaligned stance by joining the European Union. Neutrality is cheap. Finland obtained a security agreement with the United States at the same time that it was renovating its air force with American planes; then it joined the European Union. One could not find a better example of how unconcerned even the most vulnerable nonaligned countries now feel about the risks' of violating the delicate political balances that they used to work so hard to maintain. In the past, nonalignment was an advantage largely because it guaranteed exclusion from any potential future conflicts. Today, nonalignment no longer means anything, because the very concept was defined as staying out of a conflict that no longer exists.

The very relative political similarity of the nonaligned countries has no more chance of surviving into the future than that of the Eastern European nations, and the consequences of its disappearance may be similar. Now that the prudence required by the nuclear order is no longer necessary, these countries are freer to act than before, but also more alone. Nothing guarantees that what were previously stable areas under the nuclear order will be now transformed into areas of political cooperation. For many non-aligned countries, this new liberty is already accompanied, as in Eastern Europe, by two fears: that they will be forgotten by the more powerful countries, which now seems much farther away, and that their neighbors, who feel the same fears, may turn into their enemies.

The universality of these phenomena has not, however, created any commonality or convergence of interests. History has given way to anecdote, and localized concerns have acquired the status of legitimate political interests. Once forced to be clear-cut because uncertainty was intolerable, in the future political power games may once again become ambiguous.

What Foundations Are We Laying for Our Future Security?

Let us make no mistake; this general unraveling affects the very nature of collective security. Alliances are disappearing because the logic that kept them together—mutual assured destruction—has itself disappeared. Large multinational political-military organizations are a thing of the past. Nations will have to find stability elsewhere, for the very concept of a political order founded on collective security interests no longer exists. Much more than just the Cold War ended with the fall of the Berlin Wall in 1989; a certain conception of order and security that had remained unchanged for centuries also went by the board. The principle of sovereignty expressed by territory and borders dividing countries that are indifferent to each other—except when they have a common interest—is a thing of the past. Also gone is the idea of a status quo that could be defined or changed only at the whim of the great powers. The logic of certain death intensified these ideas to the point of stifling all political movement because it made them absolutely rigid. The political map of the world was frozen so that the entire planet would not freeze in a nuclear winter. This political theory was not new even if the weapons in question were.

These traditional principles of political order began to change during the Cold War, beginning with the principle of sovereignty. Even when the opposition of the East and the West carried it to extremes, other unofficial changes increasingly undermined it—changes brought about, unexpectedly, by the Cold War itself. In order to build itself up, the Western Alliance, in Europe as in Asia, encouraged back-door communication among its members and encouraged the integration of their economies. The formation of this new style of coalition, which originated in war, has become, due to the spontaneous play of national interests, a more and more powerful self-sustaining movement. The integration of national economies now seems like a naturally evolving phenomenon, hitherto limited only by the principle of sovereignty. And the whole notion of sovereignty is being overtaken by the more powerful forces of the marketplace, which are bypassing it more and more. Indeed the States themselves are assenting to this erosion of the concept of sovereignty—a concept that, all of a sudden, seems to hinder nations in their quest for wealth. In Southeast Asia as well as in Eastern Europe, Latin America, and the Middle East, countries are working toward a new world order by integrating themselves into larger groups that promise to further their economic development.

But there's more. Sovereignty must now compete not only with the pursuit of prosperity, but also with international law—yet another change from the traditional order. That order based itself on States as the sole source of both authority and law. Whatever the Powers had agreed upon together became international law. Conversely, whatever the Powers had not agreed upon was by definition revolutionary, therefore *absolutely* unacceptable. The intellectual son of Metternich, Henry Kissinger has often pointed out that it was the States which rejected this arrangement that were the most dangerous ones. In the 1960s, he repeatedly insisted that China presented—for this very reason—a greater threat than the USSR, which was a greater power but which respected international agreements even if it sometimes sought to bend them to its advantage.

This whole structure is vanishing as well. It appears that international law, like economics, is itself becoming an organizing principle in international relations. It no longer arises from the will of one or two Superpowers, but rather from a collective process, and its rules now tend to supersede those of individual States. This second breach of the sovereignty principle is particularly serious because the law as it is conceived of here is not that of States but of nations. The underlying ideal is that of a civil society on a world scale in which a now-universalized legal system would ensure harmonious integration.

The ambition of this twofold integration—of economics and of international law—represents a radical change from the previous principles of international organization. Because they bypass or diminish State sovereignties, and because they address the individual and personal needs of citizens—justice and prosperity—these integrations are becoming the organizing principles of a new world order. They seem capable of achieving an unprecedented global stability. In fact, their influences should make it considerably harder for States to impose policies that encroach on the rights of individuals. Thus conceived, such an integration would in itself constitute a world order.

But this idea is false.

CHAPTER 5

Economics:
A Natural World Order?

War with Germany is impossible. Our fortunes are too
closely linked to one another. Her destruction would also
mean the ruin of so many of our debtors that it would
entail our own ultimate ruin as well. The consequences
would be such that we could never take Germany's place on
the markets that she once controlled, even without taking
into account the loss of the German market itself.

—Norman Angell, *The Grand Illusion* (1912)

Toward a Natural Economic Order?

Defense organizations and shared security concerns no longer link
countries together. This is changing the face of the world. The vast
collective-security project that was the struggle against Communism created a political community whose commitment matched
the life-or-death character of that struggle. In order to wage this ultimate battle between the forces of light and darkness, everything
had to be mobilized and unified: moral values, political institutions,
economic principles. This was a way to give security concerns both
a universal—"the free world"—and a regional dimension. Every region of the world organized itself in order to contribute to the fight
against Communism—in the name of defending the free world as
well as in its own self-interest. These regional political structures

born out of security concerns are also fading away, at the same time that movements towards economic integration are growing.

Since the end of the 1980s, regional groupings of countries have come into vogue. Every last corner of the earth has its own free-trade zone, tax union, or common market. The globalization of economies was the fad of the 1980s; the regionalization of economies may well be the fad of the 1990s. These two trends, however, have very different political meanings. Globalization was presented as a purely economic mechanism, the inevitable triumph of the demands of business and finance over borders or diplomatic constraints. The latter were not destroyed, they were simply bypassed; economics was a world unto itself. Regional economic integrations, by contrast, can hopefully lead to better political relationships. Each such integration involves a few adjoining countries whose ambition it is to eventually arrive at an advanced form of interdependence. This way of thinking involves a logic of "always more" which, when successful, is supported by the prosperity and stability that it has created. Such an integration thus becomes a self-fulfilling prophecy.

But in the process, could not such integrations change from being economic in nature to being political? This is certainly not their goal today. At this point, the Caribbean Common Market,* the Andean Group,** the West African States with their economic group or economic community, Southeast Asia with ASEAN,† and

---

*An organization of the Caribbean Community (CARICOM), which was established by treaty in 1973. The U.S. is not a member. Members as of 1996 were Antigua, Bahamas, Barbados, Belize, Dominica, Grenada, Guyana, Jamaica, Montserrat, St. Lucia, St. Vincent and the Grenadines, Suriname, and Trinidad and Tobago. [Translator's note]

**Established in 1969 by agreement among Bolivia, Chile, Colombia, Ecuador, Peru and Venezuela. Chile withdrew in 1977. [Translator's note]

†The Association of South East Asian Nations, a regional organization formed in 1977 by the Bangkok Declaration. Member as of 1996 were Brunei, Indonesia, Malaysia, Philippines, Singapore, Thailand, and Vietnam. Cambodia, Laos, and Papua New Guinea have observer status. [Translator's note]

quite a few similar regional groupings do not appear to be trying to form federations or even stable political alliances.

Perhaps some day these groups will take an official group position on defense issues, but that is not their main concern. Thanks to their persistence and to the beginnings of prosperity and stability that they have brought, these groupings have slowly developed their own shared characteristics. The history of long-standing groups such as those of the Andes and Southeast Asia exemplify this trend. Over the past thirty years, the members of these groups have come to believe firmly that they share something particular in common. It is a kind of island mentality, a sense of difference based on geography and not on history or institutions. This results in a degree of common identity that encourages these groups to persevere, in spite of results that are often modest.

Hence the model of integration that successfully emerged from the Cold War is not that of NATO but that of the European Economic Community. Attempts at integration, first commercial and then economic, are springing up everywhere; they grow by successive lockings-on, like trains. Regional economic centers are being created, which are drawing more and more distant neighbors to them.

Integrate to Stabilize: a Strategy for the Century's End?

The creation of the EEC* owes nothing to economic spontaneity. It is the result of the need to strengthen Europe against the Soviet Union by integrating postwar Germany into it. It was, in this respect, a complementary structure to the Atlantic Alliance and NATO—which the United States encouraged in order to consolidate its European allies.

The U.S. pursued the same policy in Southeast Asia. Starting in

---

*The European Economic Community, which succeeded the Common Market. [Translator's note]

1947, the United States was able to get Japan reinstated in the world community and to create a political unit, founded on U.S. presence in the area and on common security, that transformed the region. Now independent, these countries were mobilized for joint warfare, even while their rhetoric was often that of the militant Third World. Their leaders were able to proclaim their opposition to Western exploitation as well as their anti-Americanism, even as they massacred their own populations under the guise of rooting out Communist subversion. As Henry Kissinger noted at the time, "The neutrality of nonaligned countries and even their anti-Americanism can exist only as long as the United States is physically and spiritually strong enough." The shared need for security has created a powerful regional link in Southeast Asia. As in Europe, it has united countries which history had often set against one another and which have often been extremely fragile. When these ties were formed at the beginning of the 1960s Asia was actually an economic disaster even worse than Africa.

The United States was attempting to create stable coalitions to oppose the USSR, all the while avoiding the creation of groups strong enough to become politically independent. The purely commercial nature of the EEC's beginnings in Europe, the military monopoly of NATO, and the obvious Soviet threat made this task pretty easy. In Asia, the United States took great care to prevent any political evolution of the regional institutions whose development they controlled. Again they did this with relative ease. These countries' poverty, the latent tensions between them, and the Soviet threat—exemplified by the Vietnam War—permitted them to restrict the political organization of the region to a coalition for warfare only. On the other hand, in parts of the world where there was no Soviet threat—such as the American continent—the United States opposed any grouping that could strengthen its vassals and could threaten to lessen their dependence one day. The U.S. contributed effectively to the failure of every effort at commercial integration made by the Latin American countries in the 1960s and 1970s.

In the past ten years, this American policy of divide and conquer has become completely obsolete. It is in the process of being replaced by its opposite. From now on the United States, like other powers, is encouraging regional economic integrations in order to profit from the prosperity and the stability that they bring about. There are two reasons for this reversal of policy: the success of some of these regroupings and the desire of the Superpowers to reduce their own international political and military commitments.

Economic Integration: Good Business

The success of these regional integrations has indeed been spectacular. The European Union* has been the most complete and to date the only success: it is an economic integration that has gone far beyond mere commercial unification. On average, more than two-thirds of the foreign economic activity of the member countries takes place within the Union, whether in the domains of business, tourism, or investments. The other Western European countries have all attached themselves to this magnet. Their day-to-day economic activities are already largely integrated into that of the Union. For that matter, over 75 percent of their customers, suppliers, partners, and competitors belong to the Community. The creation early in 1993 of the European Economic Area** has institutionalized this dependence: several of these countries have since joined the European Union.

A mixed collection of neighboring countries that must use the European Union as a trade partner has developed around it. Most

---

*The organization that has superseded, but has not eliminated, the European Economic Community [Translator's note]

**L'Espace économique européen (EEE) [Translator's note]

of these, especially the poorest nations, dream of belonging to the Union one day. In the meantime, each country hopes to establish privileged relations with it in order to hitch its wagon to the modern age and escape the poverty of its immediate surroundings. The stability brought about by the European Union is undeniable.

The development of East Asia has been equally impressive. Who today remembers that in 1965 the per capita GNP in Africa was 25 percent higher than in Southeast Asia, and 50 percent higher than in South Asia? In 1968 Gunnar Myrdal's 1964 Swedish book *Vår Onda Värld [Our Miserable World]* appeared in French as *La Misère des nations [The Misery of Nations]*; in it he outlined the dead-end trap in which these countries found themselves. Since then, their per capita GNP has increased 700 percent for the Four Dragons*, whose standard of living has reached that of Spain. In Indonesia, Malaysia, the Philippines, and Thailand the per capita GNP has increased 300 percent. The standard of living in Malaysia today is comparable to that of Hungary. The Asian countries have industrialized themselves on a massive scale. In 1970 barely a quarter of their exports were industrial products; today the proportion is half and often much higher. This includes some less developed countries such as China (80 percent) and traditional exporters of raw materials that they are rich in, such as Indonesia (40 percent). The commercial success of these countries is well known. Their regional integration is less known. Yet politically it is more important.

In 1992, 45 percent of the exports of the Four Dragons went to East Asia (Japan included), as did 55 percent of the exports of the ASEAN countries** and 65 percent of Chinese exports. All told, the countries of Southeast Asia realized 40 percent of their total exports

---

*South Korea, Taiwan, Singapore, Hong Kong

**Singapore, Indonesia, Malaysia, Thailand, Philippines

among themselves in 1992, versus only 24 percent in 1972.[95] This is the level of integration achieved by the EEC in 1965.* Several of these countries are even more integrated than these averages would indicate; in this respect they are equal to the main EEC countries. Singapore sells 50 percent of its exports in East Asia (as does Britain in the European Union); Thailand 50 percent (like Germany); and Malaysia 58 percent (like Italy). Their integration is even stronger as regards manufactured goods alone: 58 percent of the manufactured exports of East Asia were sold within that region in 1992, as against 50 percent in 1980 and 35 percent in 1967.[9] These figures reveal the true levels of regional integration brought about by the simultaneous development of these countries. This phenomenon is even more obvious if we look at a larger area. On the scale of the Pacific Rim countries as a whole, economic integration has now reached the same level as in the European Union.

Fully two-thirds of all exports from the Pacific Rim countries viewed as a whole are sent to one another: 50 percent for the United States, 67 percent for Japan, and more than 75 percent for the Southeast Asian countries.** These percentages have increased by 10 percent per year over the past ten years for each of these countries, which is truly remarkable. If we look at the 1980 level (from 55 percent to 60 percent depending on the country), we might have expected to find a plateau and to see differences of evolution depending on the size and the growth rate of the different countries.

The Asianization of the trade of the countries of Southeast Asia is massive. This movement goes beyond the commercial realm. This convergence of trade has been accompanied by a genuine integration that is embodied in the interlocking industrial and financial investments of each country in the others. Japan is obviously

---

*Today [1995] it's over 60 percent.

**Seventy-five percent for the Four Dragons, 76 percent for the ASEAN countries and 77 percent for China

the leader in this area. For over thirty years, Japan has invested massively in the production of the raw materials that are indispensable to its economy. For twenty years, it has planted its most polluting and space-consuming refining industries (aluminum, steel, and glass factories), on the Asian continent, and for the past ten years, it has also sent its skilled-labor industries overseas. Japan is not alone: recently Taiwan and Singapore have become the largest investors in Vietnam. Furthermore, the Chinese outside the People's Republic also constitute a rather remarkable force for regional financial integration. Since 1990, fully *one-half* of all foreign industrial investments in China have originated with those "outside" Chinese, mainly from Taiwan and Hong Kong. Factories in Hong Kong employ over 3,000,000 workers from China's neighboring Guangdong Province, whose trade with Hong Kong is equal to Hong Kong's total GNP! In 1994 Guangdong Province alone was responsible for over half the total exports of China.

Will Prosperity Create Security?

Economic and political integration were able to develop fully only once the security ties were loosened. It is also no accident that the drive toward European unification was revived in 1985, on the heels of the Cold War's last crisis, the Euro-missile conflict of 1981–1983. It is also no accident that the first discussions of political cooperation among the countries of Southeast Asia came immediately after the Russian-American military accords of 1989. No longer mortgaged to their defense budgets, and building on the success of their economic integration, these countries now committed themselves to deepening it, without neglecting the political realm.

This development was made easier by the support of the United States. On the one hand, the U.S. pragmatically realized that the economic successes of Europe and Asia were changing the world's balance of power. The U.S. also became aware that, with some exceptions, the strengthening of these links and the resulting political ties could allow it to reconcile two of its goals that until then had been mutually exclusive: to maintain stable regional alliances and at the same time to reduce its commitment to them. Their common prosperity makes stability necessary for these countries and gives them the means to contribute increasingly to the cost of their own defense.

For the Americans to continue to enjoy this happy situation, these countries must remain dependent on the United States as the ultimate guarantor of their defense. But this guarantee can be obtained in several ways. One is to make sure that certain countries will never agree to have to choose between an alliance with the United States and one with their own neighbors. This is the case today for the United Kingdom or Italy in Europe, and of Thailand or Japan in Asia. Another way is to stress the existence of security interests that only the United States can guarantee. These can be latent conflicts waiting to erupt, such as between Turkey and Greece, or major external threats, such as the invasion of Kuwait and the possible resulting cutoff of the oil supply. In the end, these countries will accept this dependence all the more easily if the day-to-day American presence remains discreet. Germany is a good example. Two out of three Germans believe that keeping a close relationship with the United States is necessary to their country's defense, but a majority of Germans would also like to see a reduction in the American military presence. That suits Washington very well.

This policy has since been systematically followed by the United States. The support that it is providing for economic integration on the American continent is one of the most obvious proofs that it has reversed its strategy since the end of the 1980s. The increase in the number of such projects is impressive indeed. In South America, the United States has arbitrated between Argentina, Brazil, Uruguay, and Paraguay. Recently, the U.S. has pushed for the establishment of the Mercado Común del Sur* or "Mercosur" in order to bring them together. Mercosur is a very ambitious program to abolish tariff barriers between these countries, which would lead to the free circulation of people and capital—as within the EEC—by 1996. On January 1, 1995, 90 percent of customs duties were eliminated between these countries; trade between them has tripled since 1991. In 1992, five Andean countries (Bolivia, Ecuador, Colombia, Peru, and Venezuela) launched the Andean Group with the goal of eliminating all import duties among themselves—and, among the last three countries, creating a true free-trade zone.

Similar efforts are under way in Central America. Here too, these initiatives have been around for a long time, but they have been limited in their effects until recently. In 1960, a regional common market was launched that permitted numerous decreases in customs duties and the development of regional commerce: the share of exports by participants that were bought within the regional market rose from 7 percent in 1960 to 22 percent in 1983, then collapsed to 12 percent in 1990. In order to stem the tide of decline, these countries, with the help of the United States, decided in July 1994 to create a free-trade zone in six years that would include Mexico, Venezuela, and Colombia. The latter three countries had already joined together in the "Group of Three" for the same purpose.

The most important such initiative, of course, was the creation in 1993 of the North American Free Trade Agreement (NAFTA), the first such enterprise in which the United States has participated as a member. The United States now sends 33 percent of its exports to NAFTA countries, while Canada and Mexico export fully 75 percent within the same organization. This creation is already be-

---

*Common Market of the South, formed January 1, 1995 by Argentina, Brazil, Paraguay, and Uruguay [Translator's note]

ginning to restructure North American commerce. The main Latin American nations are closely linked to NAFTA: 40 percent of Brazil's exports and 50 percent of Argentina's go to NAFTA states. Since 1993, the Central American trade zone has been given a new impetus to coordinate with NAFTA, with Mexico serving as the linchpin that ties the two groups together. The Central American countries maintain with NAFTA the same relations, based on dependence and hope, that the North African and Eastern European countries have developed with the EEC. They have also encountered the same problems. Canada and the United States do not want Mexico to become an open door to goods and workers from its less-developed neighbors—who, of course, practice the same "social dumping" for which the American opponents of NAFTA are already criticizing Mexico. Mexico, fully aware of the advantages of its participation, is therefore particularly vigilant toward its neighbors to the south.

This economic reorganization of the Americas seems to be to everyone's liking. United States influence has not diminished, but it is exercised in a less permanent and less direct way. Regional identities and roles have been reinforced: we have seen the first *rapprochement* between Portuguese-speaking Brazil and its Spanish-speaking neighbors, the creation of the Andean and Central American trade agreements, and Mexico's pivotal role as a link between the two worlds. Economic integration actually seems to be leading, bit by bit, to a political order in the western hemisphere.

The same strategy is being pursued elsewhere. In East Asia, the United States is cautiously exploring strengthening the regional institutions. The economic power of these countries, combined with the complexity of their interrelations, makes this a difficult task. It is still in its infancy, but there is no doubt of America's determination in this area. Economically, the United States supports the

growth of APEC* by assigning to this association increasingly detailed responsibilities: coordinating environmental policy, aid in
developing small business, rethinking maritime policies—in short
all the tasks that confirm its procedural role in the coordination of
a vast zone of economic development. Politically, the increased
number of summit meetings among the Pacific Rim countries, the
support of diplomatic initiatives by ASEAN, as well as Washington's desire to consult formally with these countries concerning
crises in the region—all these are positive signs.

The same holds true for the Middle East. There too, as the security issues in the region are slowly being resolved, an economic integration is taking shape, for the same reasons as in other areas of
the world. The massive aid that has been given to Egypt, and that
will soon be extended to Jordan, the unstinted encouragement
given to Lebanon to return to its role as a regional financial center,
the renewed interest in the French plan to have the oil-producing
states finance this development—all are unmistakable indications
of this trend. Syria is well aware of this. President Assad realizes
that the greatest risk for his country is to be left out of this movement of modernization and regional integration. Offers of substantial economic aid to Syria, and accelerated cooperation among
the other regional powers as international financing reaches them,
are powerful incentives for him to join in the transformation that
now beckons.

The policy of the United States toward the European Union both
confirms this strategy and indicates its limits. Washington decided
to support the European Union once it was convinced that it
would not adversely affect NATO, that is to say ultimate U.S. control over European defense. The best illustration of this is the fact
that the Maastricht Conference in December 1992 was preceded
by the Atlantic Alliance summit that November in Rome. That au-

---

*The Asia-Pacific Economic Co-operation Group [Translator's note]

tumn was filled with barely disguised tensions between those Europeans who strongly supported the Union (France, Germany, Belgium, Spain, Luxembourg), and the unyielding supporters of the Atlantic Alliance (the United Kingdom, the Netherlands, Italy). The former tried to obtain the strongest resolutions possible concerning the creation of a European defense policy, while the latter tried to keep this a matter for NATO only. The former put in motion spectacular initiatives, like the announcement in October of the formation of a European armed force by France and Germany. The others, who shuttled back and forth to Washington, made it clear that the success of the Maastricht Conference strictly depended on that of the Rome summit, clearly showing where their allegiance lay. . . .

Compromise was reached in coexistence and will remain there. This was clearly shown during the meeting of the French and American foreign ministers in February 1993. For the entire two hours of this meeting, the only subject discussed was the compatibility of the European Union and the Atlantic Alliance. "The Alliance will survive only if the United States accepts the creation the European Union; it will become stronger because of it, otherwise it will wither away," explained French Foreign Minister Roland Dumas. James Baker argued, "It is unacceptable to affect the integrity of NATO. It is the key to any alliance between our two continents." Dumas asked sarcastically, "NATO? What is going to happen with it, in your opinion? Tell me about 'NATO II: After the Cold War.'" Baker prudently didn't try. No one changed sides, but the lines were drawn on both sides and all parties found themselves able to adapt to the coexistence of the two views.

This strategy has become widespread. French policy in Africa is taking the same direction for the same reasons and along the same lines as United States policy in Asia. France is trying to reduce the cost of its aid, to place increased responsibility in the hands of the African nations themselves, and to foster stability by regionalizing their economic development. Paris is emphasizing the need for the African nations to take collective responsibility for meeting their own defense needs as well. In December 1994 the president of France suggested that a pan-African force be created to provide humanitarian assistance or to keep the peace on the African continent. By remaining a financial and military advisor, France hopes to reduce its monetary commitment in the region without losing its influence.

Turkey is initiating a similar policy in Central Asia. It represents half the GNP in its sphere of influence, a region that extends from Bulgaria to the borders of China and from the Caucusus to Kuwait. Turkey also exerts a strong cultural influence. As a modern Muslim and secular State, Turkey constitutes a model for numerous countries in the region, which for the most part also speak Turkic languages and follow Sunni Islam. The success of its economic development, its links to the United States, and its participation in NATO give Turkey international status in the region. Furthermore, Turkey brings a lot of economic aid into the region: $2 billion in 1992, a huge amount both for itself and for the surrounding region,* where its influence is real. All this does not, however, give Turkey either the means or the ambition to assume the role of political protector. On the contrary, Turkey has shown great discretion. It is acting as a moderator only, refusing to involve itself in regional crises and remaining on good terms with its neighbor Iran. Turkey has also remained clear about its interests: they lie in integrating with the West and not the East. Its first priority is to belong to Europe, not to Asia. Turkey is more an island than a bridge.[9] It would be wrong, then, to see Turkey's efforts as a return to its historic policy of "Greater Turkey." The concept of pan-Turkism is doubly absurd. In the first place, there is no unity, even latent unity, among the coun-

---

*Or 1.5 percent of its GNP; this would represent an investment of $90 billion for the U.S.

tries of Central Asia; in the second place, Turkey has no desire or motive to create one.

Economics and commerce have become engines that are uniting groups of extremely diverse countries. Seen in this light, the world is organized like a series of boxes, each locked on to the next. The world map is dominated by the power and density of the economic links formed by the industrialized Triad* of Japan, North America, and Western Europe.* Seventy-five percent of the business investments made by corporations outside their home countries are made in Triad countries and made by Triad corporations. The three most important stock markets—London, New York, and Tokyo— account for 80 percent of the world's financial transactions. Of the 4,000 long-term business agreements recorded between 1980 and 1995, fully 92 percent were between Triad corporations. Looking closely at each member of the Triad, we again find the same network of linkages and interdependences between the individual economic giants and the zones that surround them. A closer look at the latter zones reveals the same mechanisms at work—and so on down to the smallest economic units.

The World Order of Business Will Have to Serve a Long Apprenticeship

While these economic integrations are powerful enough to unify countries and even continents, they are incapable of bringing political adversaries together. The economic integration of the Triad is very far advanced. Even the largest country cannot oppose the free movement of capital, funds, businesses, or goods. This has not, however, led to any convergence of political policies at all. Instead we have a juxtaposition of differing democracies, and it would be diffi-

---

*Name given by Japanese management consultant Kenichi Ohmae to these three powerful industrial zones, as a group.

cult to find a political project or a cause that all the largest industrial countries have in common. They may share common interests, such as maintaining the global stability that is essential for good business, but nothing more. The economic integration of the Triad creates no convergence of policies other than the defense of the conditions that support their shared economic prosperity.

The triumph of economics does not diminish with geographic scale. Economic integrations at the continental level create no common political agenda, not even the simple affirmation of a common identity. Whenever any such attempt has been made, it has been rejected immediately. In 1992, for example, the prime minister of Malaysia proposed the creation of an "Asian Market" that would exclude non-Asians: Australians, New Zealanders, and of course Americans and Canadians. This drew a general outcry from his Asian neighbors. In the first place, they thought this was a politically dangerous idea; this was confirmed by the harshly negative reaction of the United States to the proposal. But above all, they simply could not see the point of such a move. The idea of an Asian identity has no reality for the parties concerned. Despite forty years of cooperation and twenty years of a common journey into prosperity, the disappearance of the threat they shared has led to a rapid unraveling of the political ties among these countries. Freed from the need to combat a common enemy, these countries are reviving the latent conflicts that set them against each other. Similar ethnic tensions, economic disputes, and age-old rivalries and distrust are pushing East Asia towards a fragmentation similar to Europe's.

As in Europe, there exists in Asia no common political frame of reference that would allow a unity founded on defense concerns to be converted into political cooperation or integration. To try to ascribe common political goals to a region that reaches from Bangladesh to Japan based on its economic integration would be absurd. The countries in question possess very different political regimes and traditions. Authoritarian and paternalistic systems where national unity is sought through economic prosperity (Indonesia, Brunei, Singapore) lie next door to conservative and restrictive Japanese-style democracies where economics and politics blend (Korea, Taiwan). These countries offer a sharp contrast with those whose institutions are dominated by ethnic divisions (Malaysia) or those that have attained Western-style democracy without also attaining prosperity (the Philippines).[75] The rise of Islam in the political life and legislation of Indonesia, Brunei, and Malaysia has caused more than a little friction with their large Buddhist communities. In the Philippines the Buddhists are also in competition with Roman Catholicism, the majority religion there.

Southeast Asia is unified only from a European vantage point. The Asian mosaic is actually as fragile as that of our Eastern European neighbors. Being Asian may imply a promise of economic development, but certainly not shared ideas about politics or strategy. The 50,000,000 overseas Chinese are as much interested in their homeland economically as they fear it politically. In most of the countries where they live, they constitute a powerful group; they often have strained relations with the ethnic majorities in those countries, which they dominate economically. And this domination is becoming regional. Since 1993, Taiwan has become the number one investor in most Southeast Asian countries, from Vietnam to Indonesia. Yet whatever their feelings may be towards Beijing, these Chinese are perceived as Chinese first and foremost. This tension between Chinese and non-Chinese is a high-voltage line that crosses all of Asia.

Japan is a particularly instructive case, because it is both a powerful and a pacifist integrating force. Over one-fourth of all ASEAN foreign trade goes to Japan, and vice versa. Japan also provides two-thirds of all development aid to the region. Furthermore, Japan is the source of over half of all direct financial investments in the ASEAN countries, and that share is growing. Since 1985, fully half of all Japan's foreign investments have been made in Asia.

The swift rise to the top of this economic power* has been accompanied by extreme political caution. Japan has never taken a
major initiative without the United States lighting the way. It pur-
sues diplomatic initiatives only via economic means: aid, assistance, cooperation, etc. Its leaders emphasize how reluctant the
Japanese are to commit themselves overseas politically, even for humanitarian reasons. Japanese public opinion strongly opposes any
regional political integration. The increase in development aid over
the past fifteen years was decreed by the administration: neither the
Diet nor public opinion were consulted, for fear of their refusal.
Today as in the past, over 75 percent of the Japanese public opposes this aid expansion policy. While Japan alone provides 20 percent of the development aid financed by all States to foreign
countries, the Japanese provide only 2 percent of world aid from
private sources. A law permitting the participation of unarmed
Japanese soldiers in United Nations peacekeeping troops was
passed in 1993; it set off real political convulsions, so strongly do
the Japanese oppose foreign entanglements. The Japanese government was forced to amend the text's language so that it did not require the actual approval of the Diet, but only acceptance by the
government committees concerned.

Japan is trying to look like a responsible and unified State, but a
State that is pacifist and without ambition except in the economic
arena. It is on this basis that Japan defends its candidacy for a permanent seat on the Security Council. Since 1983, Japan has proclaimed itself the Asian representative to the Group of Seven,
which comprises the seven principal industrial powers. Since 1986,
Japan has argued for an increased role for small nations at the
United Nations and for a less military concept of security, which it
feels it exemplifies well in Asia. Since 1992, Japan has maintained
that there is no reason for military powers to continue to dominate

---

*Japan's GNP was 25 percent less than West Germany's in 1960, equal to West
Germany's in 1968, and twice as large in 1990.

the UN Security Council, since economic power has now become more dominant to world affairs. By saying this, Japan is attempting to transform economic integration into political logic.

This altruism and prudence have done little to reassure Japan's neighbors. Whether or not the United States would be Japan's guarantor is also of little moment; every new move on the part of Japan to affirm itself and take on more responsibility on the international scene is seen as a step in its supposed plan to reconquer Asia, even by such far-off countries as India. The slow transformation of its economic integration into a political order centered in Japan is being fought by the whole of Asia, all the more vehemently as its economic integration is growing. Japan and its neighbors are involved in a struggle in which time is of the essence; and time is working against Japan. That is why Japan has fought so hard to join the Security Council. Its special claim to represent Asia on the Council is in fact losing legitimacy on two fronts.

On the political front, it is clear that Japan cannot assume any federating role; its neighbors' emotions run too high, their suspicion is too visceral. After all is said and done, Japan remains extremely isolated. Its leaders are realizing, not without bitterness, that their role in the region is accepted only because they have money. Time is also working against Japan on the economic front. Its dominance in the region is steadily decreasing: in 1992 it represented 25 percent of ASEAN trade versus 37 percent in 1980, 11 percent of the trade of the Four Dragons versus 16 percent in 1980, and 13 percent of China's trade versus 25 percent in 1978. Japan's financial dominance, remains overwhelming, but it has never been able to create a "yen zone"; only 15 percent of all Japan's imports are paid for in yen.

Southeast Asia is linked together by powerful common interests, but certainly not by any values capable of supporting a political order. Whatever political unity may have existed in the past is fraying as I write; it was imposed entirely from the outside by the Soviet threat and the intense American presence. The disappearance of these factors is uncovering divisions faster than it is creating ways to overcome them.

The same is true of Europe. It took the EEC forty years before it was able to even contemplate becoming a political union, and it looks as though it will need at least as many more to get there. On the continental scale, "European identity" remains a myth that everyone gives lip service to but no one really accepts. Both the confederation proposed by France and the "common house" of Europe advocated by Russia have been rejected by the very Eastern European countries that were supposed to have been their principal beneficiaries. These abstract affirmations of common values and these new political "mechanisms" neither interest those countries nor bring them closer together.

Even on a smaller scale, political goals remain limited. The ASEAN countries, for example, share something in common with their neighbors and partners. Their awareness of this, combined with shared economic interests, is strong enough to allow these countries to make plans together. In 1991, for the first time, they created a free-trade zone with the modest goal of reducing tariffs among themselves by 5 percent in fifteen years. There are two reasons for this caution. The first reason is that the economic reality of the ASEAN common market, like that of other restricted markets of developing countries, is rather weak. Although these countries do 75 percent of their business within the Pacific Rim, only 5 percent of it is done among themselves—a percentage that has remained unchanged over the past fifteen years. The second reason is that although the ASEAN countries may be different from the countries outside of ASEAN, that does not mean that they resemble one another. These countries are separated by sharp contrasts; there are even political, ethnic, or religious conflicts between them. They have no common ground on which to found a common political association, and so far they have refrained from doing so.

In the end, economic integration seems capable of leading to political ties only on a very modest scale. Scandinavia is one example. The Caribbean, too, has had a common market since 1960 that groups together the region's often minute island States. In spite of different levels of success, this project has been continued for thirty years because it fulfills at least two basic needs. One, actually secondary, is economic. The goal for these countries is to achieve a maximum amount of self-sufficiency and development. They have been able to double the share of the business that they do among themselves (from 4.5 percent in 1960 to slightly over 10 percent at the end of the 1980s), but it will be difficult for this progress to continue. These countries are too small and not complementary enough to manage that. This is not to say that the attempt has been a failure, since the other goal of this common market is their real priority. This goal consists in establishing, if not a group identity, then at least some form of group specificity, since the Caribbean is neither fully North American nor fully Central American. The Caribbean islands share strong and original characteristics—historical, ethnic, and geographical.

Even on such a small scale, even with common histories and interests, nothing assures that nations will come together. The inability of the little Baltic States to form a federation is one sad example. The pan-Arab nation has failed to become a political reality for over thirty years, thus showing that a strong feeling of belonging is not enough to form a political entity—even with a common language, a common religion, a common ethnicity, and, until the last few years, even a common enemy.

Economic Integration: an Effect, Not a Cause

Economic integration, then, can at best bring about only limited political integration. This is true especially since there are more poor countries in the world than wealthy ones. Between the zones of regional integration that have developed in recent years lie vast hinterlands of disorganization and disunity. Sub-Saharan Africa is the most conspicuous example. Its 500 million inhabitants represent 10 percent of the world's population, but 50 percent of its people who live in destitution.

Over the past twenty years, the per capita GNP in sub-Saharan Africa has *decreased* by 13 percent, whereas it has increased by 31 percent in the rest of the developing countries. One African out of two is poorer today than in 1963. The same is true for "only" one Latin American out of four and one Asian out of twenty. And there is no reason to be optimistic, if only for demographic reasons. In the past twenty-five years the population of Africa and the rest of the developing nations has doubled. In the next twenty-five years it will double again in Africa, whereas in other developing countries it will only increase by 50 percent, a rate that will continue to slow down.

Other regions now face or will face similar difficulties. South Asia, for example, has a population of 1.2 billion people. Its per capita wealth is almost as low as sub-Saharan Africa's, and its 43 percent of people living in absolute poverty is comparable. Unlike sub-Saharan Africa, however, South Asia is developing. While the per capita GNP has decreased in Africa since 1965, it has doubled in South Asia. Subsistence farming has made enormous progress and the distribution of wealth has become slightly less inequitable; as a result the quality of life in Asia is noticeably better. Furthermore, as noted above, the rate of population increase has been decreasing measurably there over the past thirty years, whereas it has continued to increase in Africa.

Central Asia is a third example of this type of hinterland. The geographical concept of "Central Asia" itself is back in fashion, as it was from the thirteenth to the eighteenth century. It encompasses the ex-Soviet republics to the east of the Caucasus, between the Caspian Sea and China, and includes 50,000,000 people with an estimated per capita GNP of $1,200 in 1989 but only $600 in

1992.[60] Even the higher of these two figures would place these countries only on a par with Guatemala and Congo. And such a measure may well prove optimistic, given the serious problems that these countries are experiencing. The same is true of the republics of the Caucasus, where the economic conditions are similar (a per capita GNP of $1,200 in 1989 and $870 in 1992) and the political conditions are even worse.

These massive economic failures are always accompanied by political breakups. This correlation is worth emphasizing. As we saw in Southeast Asia, prosperity does not always create political closeness. Economic collapse, on the other hand, is always accompanied by political fragmentation. Sometimes for good reason. In Africa, for example, this has been due in part to the increasing contrast between the countries committed to democratization and the others. But that's not the main reason for it. The main reason is still poverty—and the perverse but strong link between poverty and disorder. In all the large poverty zones, political and economic collapses happen simultaneously. Today's world economic integrations thus are leaving stranded half of the world's people, whose misery is forcing them into very hostile relations with their neighbors.

A world political order created from the integration of the world's economies is still a long way off. It will not suddenly come into being just because it is needed: Africa and Eastern Europe prove this. All the regions where economic integration could lead to a political order are regions where such an order already exists: Latin America, East Asia, Western Europe. All these areas were held together by the Cold War and American domination.

Even when it is successful, this integration can have no political consequences that are capable of contributing to our collective security. That is what is happening right now in Asia. When all the factors for success are finally brought together, the transformation from economic integration to political order takes place only at the slow pace of the evolution of species. . . .

Economic mechanisms function in a hermetically sealed system: all they do is integrate economies. And yet many believe otherwise. We often invest our principal rivals' economic integrations, in Asia for example, with political virtues or prospects that they cannot possess. The imperatives of national security no longer produce political rationality, but those involved in economics are unaware of all that. The forces of business and finance are becoming more and more indifferent to States. Closed off, States are condemned to a fatal marginalization; opened up, they are subjected to the inexorable laws of economic competition.

CHAPTER 6

International Law
as a Utopia

—OK, so what do you do when there's a war?

—We open a file; we have a meeting; we write a press release
in which we communicate our heartfelt regret.

—And if the war continues?

—In that case, we play hardball: we form a committee and
sometimes even a subcommittee and we request the bel-
ligerents to end the carnage.

—And if the war continues?

—Then we send a recommendation, not a request. Do you
see the nuance? I'm not afraid to send one, a real recommendation.

—And if the war continues?

—Then we express our wishes: while siding with the weaker
party, we nevertheless do not blame the stronger. We ask
both countries to solemnly declare that they are not waging war, but rather setting in motion peace maneuvers;
that's much more peaceful. In general, military operations come to an end eventually. We permit the stronger
party to take whatever territory it desires, as long as the
word "annexation" is never spoken. For in spite of whatever hack journalists looking for a story may say, we are
not utopians.

—Albert Cohen, *Mangeclous* (1938)

The Rise of International Law

For the last several hundred years, war and the law have been in competition. Each in turn has ruled the world, more and more widely. And the law seems to be winning out. States have become increasingly willing to submit their actions to the rule of law. Traditionally a legal order has reflected a political order, and not the other way around. A legal order reflected force and territory. The Enlightenment invented the idea of Natural Law, that is to say elements of law that are universal. The extension and acceptance of this idea over the course of the nineteenth century and the beginning of the twentieth are often cited as indications of the progress of civilization. However, this reality should be qualified. On the one hand, this advance of civilization was simply the advance of colonialism. On the eve of World War I, 97 percent of the world's States were either colonizers or—mostly—colonized. On the other hand, this acceptance of the concept of natural law remained for a long time a matter of good intentions only. Not only have natural laws seldom become official laws, but even when they were made official they never wielded any real political power, as illustrated by the failure of the League of Nations.

But since 1945, and especially since 1990, the situation has changed. For the first time, States are searching for a balance between maintaining their national sovereignty on the one hand and, on the other, subjecting all nations to consistent, universal principles. Respect for international law has become the foremost of these principles and States have the obligation to respect it. As a result, these principles are not expressed solely in documents like the Declaration of the Rights of Man. From now on, they are given specific application by precisely worded, restrictive legal documents that form a tighter and tighter net. The system of international law is no longer content with stating its principles; it wants them to be actually adhered to as well. The system is changing from one of laws to one of regulations. Its organization is firming up and is becoming a real administrative system. This evolution began in 1945 with the creation of the United Nations. Since then, specialized UN organizations have been given responsibility for managing important aspects of international life, such as the mails, telecommunications, maritime traffic, meteorology, and many others. These technical organizations came first, but on the political level the desire for universal laws already existed. The system of the United Nations expressed this desire from the outset. It sought to acquire the tools it would need to anticipate and resolve any international crisis that could then be imagined.

The United Nations sought to resolve commercial problems by creating GATT,* problems of international economic organization with the creation of the IMF,** those of underdevelopment with the creation of the World Bank, the UNIDO†, the UNDP‡ and other economic programs. Besides, all the conflicts of sovereignty—and thus of security—were supposed be solved by the General Assembly and the Security Council of the United Nations.

Although the UN never even came close to achieving this ambition, the success of the international technical organizations has been, overall, exemplary. Their success has facilitated the acceptance of international regulations and regulatory bureaus. Because their authority is recognized, these organizations have been able to map out an international legal system that overrides political divisions. Conversely, they seemed to show that the only obstacle to the worldwide acceptance of such a legal system was the fact that the world was divided into two opposing blocs. The disappearance of these blocs was welcomed because it seemed to remove the last

---

*The General Agreement on Tariffs and Trade [Translator's note]

**International Monetary Fund [Translator's note]

†United Nations Industrial Development Organisation

‡United Nations Development Programme.

remaining obstacle to placing the entire domain of international relations under the rule of law.

Without waiting for such a glorious outcome, this utopian law went right on evolving throughout the Cold War years. Convinced that international law would someday become a force for world-wide political integration, its advocates worked tirelessly to cast their net wider and pull it tighter. They affirmed very powerful concepts that little by little gave international law enormous power. Thus at the 1969 Vienna Convention on Treaties the concept of "an *imperative* norm of international law" was introduced. Similarly, in the mid 1960s, the International Court of Justice and the European Commission imposed the precedence of European Community law over national law. Over the years these transfers of State power to an international legal system have weakened national sovereignty in the name of the law. This evolution has been greatly encouraged by the success of the international organizations. As they went about their work, each of these organizations has acquired a body of legal precedents in its area that has progressively confirmed its specialized competence and its legal authority over participating States. GATT is one of the best examples of this.

In the beginning, in 1945, GATT wasn't even an organization. GATT is an acronym for "General Agreement on Tariffs and Trade." It was, therefore, only an agreement, its application monitored by a small team of bureaucrats. Furthermore, it was a provisional agreement only, pending the formation of a specialized agency of the United Nations—which was finally formed fifty years later, in 1995. The growth of GATT in such arid conditions is a powerful example of the conquering march of international law. GATT had no legal authority at all. Yet year after year, its bureaucrats defined more and more legal principles and got them accepted during the course of the conflicts or debates in which it was involved. Together with the discreet but steady growth of its activities, this increasing legal application and implementation of the

GATT treaty eventually led to the de facto formation of an actual international commerce organization that continually expanded its reach, both in its membership and in its jurisdiction. GATT had only 23 member states in 1947, but 117 in 1995. Although it was originally intended to deal only with tariff issues, it first enlarged its scope to nontariff issues (quotas, allotments, and other restrictions on commerce), then to the whole field of protectionist measures.

GATT is the purely empirical creation of a legalistic world order—crowned, in 1994, by its transformation into an official international institution. This represents a symbolic consecration of international law. A half-century ago, the UN's international organizations were created to define and to impose legal rules on States. Today it is international law itself that generates institutions.

Law Enters the World of Politics

This remarkable success is not unique. The area of human rights saw an equally remarkable growth, combining a stricter and stricter codification of its principles with a permanent broadening of the scope of their application. In forty years, an enormous body of texts and institutions has been created. Starting in 1947 with the UN's International Labour Organization and UNESCO, the universal applicability of human rights law has been affirmed. The Council of Europe was formed in 1949, and an agreement on fundamental rights and liberties was signed in 1950. In 1968, the standing Arab Commission on Human Rights was established, followed in 1969 by an Inter-American Human Rights Agreement, which was expanded in 1978; a similar agreement was signed for Africa in 1981 and expanded in 1986, etc. During the same twenty-year period, over 20 international agreements and over 150 specialized international legal documents were drafted and adopted, plus any number of more or less solemn declarations. Although they were not always effective, the very accumulation of these texts strengthened the acceptance of a universal system of human rights law. Countless tenacious and patient actions of the kind over half a century have plotted out the precise limits of the sovereignty of States. Long secure in themselves, States have finally begun to recognize that their adherence to international law in the conduct of their foreign relations is not without consequences for them at home. Even on their own territory, States no longer have absolute authority. The barrier of sovereignty has become increasingly porous under the pressure of international law.

The Soviet Union learned this lesson the hard way following the 1975 conference that established the Conference on Security and Co-operation in Europe (CSCE). Like GATT at its beginnings, the CSCE was nothing but a group of texts and a procedure for discussing how to implement them. At the start this conference just looked like a confidence game where the Westerners would be taken to the cleaners, victimized by their confidence in international law—a confidence that seemed completely misplaced when dealing with such an adversary. The exchange seemed uneven, to say the least. In the agreement setting up the CSCE, the Western European countries committed themselves to opening up real political cooperation with the USSR: in real terms, this meant that they officially accepted the partition of Europe and Soviet dominance over half of it. For its part, the USSR agreed to respect certain basic human rights having to do with freedom of expression and belief. This seemed like a bad joke, given the USSR's demonstrated lack of interest in keeping such agreements after signing them—starting with the United Nations Charter.

Many saw this agreement as a pitiful charade put together by the West to mask its weakness in the face of Brezhnev's USSR. The Western countries were still reeling from the shock of the 1973 oil crisis; Nixon had been forced to resign after Watergate in 1974, and in 1975 the United States had abandoned Indochina to Moscow's allies. The legal provisions of the CSCE reinforced this impression of a con game. On the one hand these agreements had no binding force; they were only declarations of intent. On the other hand, the final act of the Conference was to strongly affirm a broad concept of State sovereignty: the respect of "rights inherent in" sovereignty (Article 1), the inviolabiity of borders (Article 3), territorial integrity (Article 4), and nonintervention in internal affairs (Article 6). Only after these do we find freedom of thought (Article 7) and the right of peoples to self-determination (Article 8).

To everyone's surprise, the text of this agreement turned out to be a formidable catalyst for the opposition movements in Eastern Europe and the USSR. Over and over again, dissidents took their arguments from the document and used them to defend their legitimacy. Its commitment to distribute the document as widely as possible and its recent signing made it difficult for the government of the USSR to silence its opponents when they demanded that the provisions of the document be applied to them. The West quickly realized this, and harassed the USSR and its vassals into keeping their promises. Taken literally, these were actually very far-reaching and biased against the USSR. The West's commitments to respect borders, resolve conflicts without violence, and preserve the political status quo in Europe did not cost it anything, since it had long ago given up waging war on Moscow. But for the Soviet, actions formerly considered interference in their internal affairs, for example demanding freedom of expression for the opposition, now became a simple matter of citing commitments that they had freely and recently made.

Undoubtedly in Stalin's USSR such a document would have been ignored; indeed, it would never have been signed. In 1975, however, the desire to look honorable (at least on paper), which is a by-product of the law, and the desires to achieve détente and to maintain the status quo had become priorities. Still today, former dissidents who have since become leaders underscore the considerable importance of the CSCE as a weapon in their battles at the end of the 1970s.

Thus the legal order was able to make itself felt even in the midst of the Cold War. It was not strong enough to transform itself into a political entity, but it was already too strong to be ignored, even by the most defensive and unwavering conception of sovereignty. States could oppose this or that application of the law at home, but such opposition increasingly led to their being marginalized at the international level.

From International Law to Utopian Law

This latent power to induce compliance was unleashed completely by the disappearance of the Soviet empire. There are catalysts that can precipitate the transformation of a liquid or even a gas into a solid. The fall of the Berlin Wall had the same effect on the global legal system. Whichever faction had international law on its side won out. Now international law could become a truly global political reality and could claim to serve as the foundation of a planetary order that would be more just than the vanished one based on the security of States. From 1988 on, Mikhail Gorbachev declared before the General Assembly of the United Nations, "Our ideal is an international community of legitimate States." In 1991, commenting on his victory over Iraq, George Bush echoed this sentiment. "No country can claim this victory as their own. It's a victory for the community of nations and the rule of law." Politicians began to dream of a world where law would set limits on every type of conflict and prevent them from flaring up at all. From now on law is everywhere, law is everything. The system of international law regulates commercial confrontations, orchestrates world economic integration, limits expulsions, and aids development. Law promotes the values of universal human rights through an astounding multiplicity of documents and agencies. Law no longer just develops out of circumstances: all of these endeavors are pieces of an enormous structure that is trying to include in its jurisdiction everything there is.

Such an ambition is possible today because the fall of the Berlin Wall has opened up to the legal system the one door previously closed to it: that leading to defense. From now on, the international legal system's priority lies in organizing peace, moderating armed conflicts, and limiting both their development and their weaponry. The United Nations and its Security Council are trying their best to become a directorate that would apply the United Nations Charter as literally as possible. In the same way, the CSCE is trying to move on from the status of moral tutor to its members to become a full-blown institution in charge of European security. In 1994, the CSCE changed its name from "Conference" to "Organization": the OSCE. It created and funded permanent divisions, some to be watchdogs of democracy and others to predict, then control international crises. The ambitions of these international organizations, heretofore powerless, show us the entire evolution of international law: from simple moral reminder to true political authority.

This authority is attempting to extend itself into the areas that are most sensitive for States. For example, legal instruments are created or strengthened to limit the proliferation of the most dangerous weaponry—nuclear, chemical, or biological—as well as the means to produce them. The underlying principles had been established long ago: the ban on chemical weapons was actually passed in 1922. Today, however, a full system for monitoring them is being put in place. This shows a determination to impose detailed regulations in order to prevent an arms race involving weapons of mass destruction—a considerable broadening of the political role of law into the area of conflict resolution.

For example, a system to monitor missile exports has been in place since 1987: the Missile Technology Control Regime (MTCR). This system doesn't simply discourage the export of weapons exceeding a certain power or range. It also carefully outlines the types of components or parts that can be sold separately, to prevent the reassembly of weapons whose sale when intact is forbidden. The MTCR goes so far as to proscribe technical cooperation as well as the sending of experts or advisors to countries that want but are forbidden these weapons. The document is very broad.

These strengthened laws demonstrate that, to a remarkable extent, States now accept such limitations on their sovereignty. The chemical-weapons interdiction treaty signed in 1993 pushes even further in this direction. The 120 signatories agreed that any one of them might make a surprise visit to any civil or military installation located in any other of them, on the mere suspicion of the existence of a chemical-weapons laboratory or factory, even an industrial one. The acceptance of such a severe curtailing of sovereignty in the name of an international treaty written by an ad hoc administration in The Hague is a major political event. It can be fairly compared to the acceptance by States of the near-inquisitorial powers of the International Monetary Fund to evaluate their economic situation. But here the issue is weaponry and security.

Sovereignty is losing power in all areas. The States are bartering its reduction for integration into the world order that this legal system is weaving together. This bartering of sovereignty for integration into the world order is a fundamental characteristic of the strategy of today's utopian international law, which hopes to create in this way a lasting political order. A serious mistake.

Legal Integration Is Not a Political Order

It is dangerous to believe that the multiplication of regulations and commitments is slowly building up some sort of super-State of international law. It is true that the world powers herald its arrival and that the United Nations creates the illusion of a proper framework for it. Some see such a powerful force in this empire of international law that they are prophesying that the State of the Law will replace Democracy as the new Holy Grail of the world's peoples.[77] This utopian legalism shows a profound confusion of the apparatus of administration with a political organization.

In fact, what we are losing is our sense of what politics really is. Institutions and laws cannot create political legitimacy; they are the results of it. This means that legal integration alone cannot found a truly secure order, and its capacity is limited to guaranteeing minimum stability only. Such a role would assume a certain consensus on what the political priorities are and on the means of achieving them. This is essential if theoretical principles are to be transformed into practical and effective measures. The battle against the proliferation of weapons of mass destruction proves this. The body of rigorous principles that is the weapon in this battle is the result of a strong political consensus, yet nuts-and-bolts regulations are few and far between. Whether discussing human rights issues, arms sales, or defense policies, the firmness of the underlying principles contrasts sharply with the vagueness of the regulations. This leads to the proliferation of a body of so-called "soft laws" whose very nature indicates both wishful thinking and powerlessness. Given the lack of a political vision that is shared by the States concerned, such a situation is hardly surprising. It is futile to believe that common interests will be a sufficient substitute for such a vision. Common interests are always more long-term than conflicting ones.

The debates surrounding world trade regulation are a good example of this. The United States agrees with the doctrine of free trade and profits from its spread, but is not particularly happy to see free-trade zones governed by an independent international organization. The U.S. finally accepted the transformation of GATT into an international organization, but Congress insisted that the U.S. retain the right to retaliate unilaterally. Washington wants to be able to substitute its own laws for supranational laws whenever it thinks it necessary.

Similarly, supervision of the most sophisticated weaponry is in the best interest of the arms exporters, since these same weapons could one day be used against their own troops. The 1991 French initiative in this area led nowhere, except to a sales catalogue produced by the UN, now transformed into a trade agency of sorts. Yet the French initiative only involved the adoption of "general restraining principles" by the five major arms exporters. At the most, each country involved would have committed itself to allow the others to make comments and to ask questions about this or that announced export. But the United States was eager to profit from the huge arms showcase that the Gulf War provided for it. France and the United Kingdom did not intend to let the U.S. keep all the profits for itself. And China did not intend to give up a convenient way to finance its military expenditures or the political leverage of being the provider of arms to countries that were closed to Western suppliers. As for Russia, she was in need of hard currency. The only shared goal of the half-dozen meetings that took place between the five countries was for each one to keep its maneuvering room in the markets where it had an advantage and to limit the advantages of the others where they were most competitive.

The European Union, or Utopia Dissolved by Reality

Nothing illustrates more dramatically the specificity of the political order than the difficulties encountered by the European Union. The construction of the Community represents an unprecedented attempt at integration. Forty years of nonstop efforts have brought its members together in an extraordinary diversity and density of ties. The passage from Community to Union is based on the idea that such a deep integration will inevitably lead to political integration as well. When two-thirds of all trade and half of all the national regulations of the twelve member States are linked to the Community that they form, when they have reached the point of

integrating their police forces and are no longer debating their for-
eign-trade policies—even at the height of the GATT crisis—then
we can assume that the critical threshold has been reached. At this
level, we might reasonably assume that legal and economic integration would also lead to political integration. Yet this is not so.
Giant steps forward, such as economic and monetary union, can
be achieved without any similar political union ensuing. At the end
of the day, the European nations are realizing that the transformation of an economic integration, no matter how advanced, into a
political order is not something to take for granted.

The strongest conflicts concern national security issues. It is revealing that eleven countries can agree more easily on the integration of their economies than on how to begin coordinating their
defense policies. In the long term, the inability to build a common
security policy will be fatal to the Union. Indeed, only the building
of such a policy can stop the renationalization of security policies
that is now taking place. If each country in the Union considers
only itself, it will have excellent reason to let the crises of its neighbors run their courses without feeling obliged to prevent or intervene in them. At best, we will see a repeat performance of the
example of Yugoslavia, where France's mobilization brought in
some other countries but not enough to be able to control the situation. At worst, and most probably, the British attitude of indifference will spread. Troublemakers will be encouraged by the
assurance of impunity, to the extent of possibly doing grave harm
to the interests of a major European State, or worse . . .

It is hard to imagine that economic integration will be able to
long survive major policy differences in matters of security when,
in the wake of a crisis, each country would feel abandoned or betrayed by the others. Inevitably, the legitimacy of the entire community's ties would be called into question. Dealing with crises
nationally will invariably lead to political tension between member
States with divergent interests: no obligation or tradition will arise
to overcome these tensions. Opportunistic alliances and tactical

games will resurface, and nationalistic emotions will once again make themselves heard.

Without Political Order, Legal Order Is Just a Band-Aid

The absence of a common political vision, then, severely limits the powers of a legal integration—even one as advanced as the European Union. This is truer still in other regions of the world where such a union is still a dream. In matters of security especially, this utopian legal system does not have the means to attain its goals, and has great difficulty in acquiring such means. It is one thing to accept the creation of a global authority to administer the mails or the allocation of telecommunications frequencies worldwide. It is quite another to accept that an international agency has the right to look into whether or not commitments in sensitive domains (such as security) are being respected. Day-to-day experience is showing that the international legal system is having a difficult time enforcing the laws that it makes. It is not just that the legal net is still too loose and still being woven. It is very unlikely that it can ever be tightened up enough to make it work as it was supposed to.

We have to leave Utopia behind and open our eyes. The most significant part of our current global monitoring system was created when a strong political order existed, one where the major powers wanted to prevent any serious crisis that might have led to a dramatic confrontation between them. In the process, of course, these nations also solidified their position as world leaders. This is how the battle against nuclear proliferation was born. The International Atomic Energy Agency, which supervises nuclear materials, was created in 1948; the Treaty on the Non-Proliferation of Nuclear Weapons (NPT) was signed in 1968; since 1973 the atomic powers have monitored the sale of the technologies that aid in building nuclear weapons. All of this illustrates the double objective of stability (preventing the proliferation of nuclear weapons) and supremacy (conserving a monopoly of them). The absence of a political order and the resulting renationalization of security interests make it ever harder to continue these types of programs, even though they are becoming more and more necessary.

Because in the end the logic of politics prevails. We must not lull ourselves with illusions. When grand alliances disappear, so do grand-scale security negotiations. There will be no more disarmament treaties in the future, and no more restrictive accords meant to forestall new crises. It will no longer be possible to sign major international security treaties like those signed at the beginning of the 1990s; it is no coincidence that the last three such treaties were all concluded within three years. In 1991 the European disarmament treaty was signed, reducing the number of major armaments (planes, tanks, helicopters, cannons, etc.) by over 100,000. In 1992, the Treaty on Conventional Forces in Europe (CFE) was signed, as well as the "Open Skies" treaty, which authorizes its signatories to make reconnaisance overflights in each other's air space to detect abnormal military operations. Finally, in 1993 a chemical weapons interdiction treaty was signed, which bans production and stocking of chemical weapons anywhere in the world. Along with the 1968 nuclear nonproliferation treaty (NPT), these four treaties constitute the basic restrictive security commitments that protect world peace today.

The force of these recent treaties derives from the fact that they are founded on the only original strategic concept since nuclear deterrence, the principle of *transparency*. The concept of transparency recognizes the fact that a security commitment is more credible when it is verifiable. While this is a basic idea, its consequences are revolutionary. It means that the word of a State is not enough; this is a direct attack on the concept of sovereignty. At the time of the NPT this idea did not yet exist. The treaty therefore did not provide for any means of verification: thus Iraq was able to violate with impunity a treaty it had signed.

The principle of transparency is becoming a reality through various declarations, measures, and verifications. In each area, each signatory makes an inventory of its stocks, which it distributes to the others. Then the commitments made are quantified for every item on the inventories; they can be inspected without prior notice by any of the member countries to verify compliance. When conceived and executed in such a way, defense treaties become extremely powerful and deserve their name.

Let's stop believing in the love of peace and the law. These treaties are the fruit of long tests of political strength and they owe their existence to powerful alliances. For practical reasons, first and foremost. Those alliances were highly structured forums with a collective negotiating discipline. Then for political reasons. The grand alliances represented the core of world power, especially if we include their client States. And the principal States on both sides were persuaded to use this power in the service of stability and disarmament. Their agreement, like their former strife, had a decisive effect on the negotiations and on compliance by third-party countries. As for the latter, the internal solidarity that each alliance demanded was able to impose the concessions needed to conclude these treaties. The European allies leaned very hard on the Americans to get them to allow their territory to be overflown within the framework of the "Open Skies" treaty. This is the first time in history that the United States has given up the idea that its territory is sacrosanct. All the leverage of their major-power patrons was needed to convince the countries of southeastern Europe (Bulgaria and Romania from the Eastern bloc, Greece and Turkey from the Western bloc) to accept some degree of disarmament. Being extremely wary of one another and having already experienced serious tensions at the end of the 1980s, these countries at first had rejected these proposals utterly.

In the future, the renationalization of defense policies will necessitate ad hoc agreements between those nations that are willing to make them. This is already the case with the Missile Technology

Control Regime (MTCR), the system that controls the export of ballistic missiles and missile parts. This is a voluntary, limited political structure. Common principles have been established and lists of sensitive products have been drawn up, regarding which all parties have agreed to exercise the greatest caution and to inform the others of their actions. Nothing is actually forbidden; any country could get around the rules if it wanted to. This type of system works because the member countries have agreed to submit to a discipline that is political in nature, not legal. The participants are not creating an institution or a list of regulations. The success of such free-will agreements is in marked contrast to the continued decline in power of the formal instruments of the international legal system. The difference lies in the fact that the former are founded on a political association that its members *want,* while the latter are not.

In the absence of a strong political order, such agreements are the best that we can make. They are the equivalent, in fact, of creating a limited political order with a specific, limited objective. They are not enough to guarantee minimum stability, because their voluntary nature limits their effectiveness. The MTCR, for example, has expanded from seven to twenty-four members, but many other countries with missile export capability still have not joined it. North Korea has sold hundreds of Scuds to Iraq and Iran and helped them to manufacture their own. China has sold medium-range missiles to Pakistan and very-long-range missiles to Saudi Arabia. This last transaction clearly illustrates the political weaknesses of such limiting agreements. The delivery and installation of missiles of this size is a very cumbersome, large-scale operation, even without taking into account the digging out of a dozen silos and the creation of a base from the ground up. And yet this was done without the knowledge of the United States, a country with close ties to Riyadh. Most ironically of all, the missile-purchase negotiations were led by the Saudi ambassador to the United States!

Volunteer organizations like the MTCR, which do not spring from a political order, will meet with only limited success. They cannot hope to impose their rules on States that decide to ignore them, whether by buying weapons or by selling them.

The fact that these supplier regimes have effectively formed a club only makes this weakness worse. Those suppliers that decline to join the club benefit from not joining, as the example of China demonstrates. This game is possible because these rules do not reflect a political order strong enough to penalize anyone who flouts it. China may be acquiring a detestable reputation, but she finds that a small price to pay for the financial and even political advantages that she is gaining. As the only seller, she names her price, creates allegiances, and uses her ability to make trouble as a bargaining chip in dealing with the other great powers. Furthermore, these clubs are dangerously reminiscent of Apartheid: *Whites Only.* This is not particularly surprising, since most of the suppliers are industrialized nations. Just the same, to the extent that the reality of present-day arms sales results not from a recognized international political order but from the concerted decisions of powerful States, the countries of the South feel themselves to be the victims of an imperialist doctrine. They clearly demonstrated this after the Gulf War when they blocked the reform of the International Atomic Energy Agency—the organization principally charged with halting trafficking in nuclear materials.

And yet conditions were ideal. Thanks to the UN sanctions imposed on Iraq after its defeat, it was possible to prove that Iraq had violated the Nuclear Non-Proliferation Treaty. Iraq had secretly acquired a complete nuclear military industry and was well on its way to building its first atomic weapon. Experts from information agencies and nuclear weapons laboratories who examined this information with the diplomats were flabbergasted by the extent and the advanced level of the Iraqi program. No one had believed that such a monumental program could have been developed clandestinely. But the evidence—including plans for nuclear weapons—was irrefutable. Such proofs are almost never obtained because such painstaking investigations are needed to collect them. The discovery of the extent of the Iraqi deception proved that the international monitoring system was a sieve. This is hardly surprising in view of the modest size of its budget, which is smaller than the U.S. Department of Agriculture's budget for animal disease control![61]

The Superpowers therefore asked that the IAEA's control mechanisms be strengthened and its mission broadened. Its *only* role, in fact, is to monitor the stocks of fissionable materials and their use.* The agency serves absolutely no other purpose. This very limited mandate has two troublesome consequences. The first is that most nuclear inspections are done in developed countries with many nuclear reactors, such as Japan and Germany, because they have a lot of nuclear material. Yet obviously these are not the most dangerous countries. The second is that this mandate precludes any police role for the agency: it is not empowered to perform any searches of suspicious installations in sovereign States without their approval. The IAEA depends entirely on the good faith and goodwill of its members since it may inspect only the installations that they declare to it. And it can do absolutely nothing against nonmembers, as North Korea was until 1994. The case of Iraq shows that the agency really is not an effective weapon to combat nuclear proliferation. For the IAEA to be truly effective, it must restructure its monitoring function and acquire the right to conduct investigations. Only then can it perform a true police function.

The principal powers in the IAEA had requested precisely these changes at the spring 1992 agency meeting that followed the Gulf War. The need for them appeared irrefutable, and they would serve

---

*The only countries not so monitored are those without nuclear installations or those that have not signed an accord with the Agency, as well as the five "officially" recognized (by the NPT) nuclear military powers: the United States, Russia, China, the United Kingdom, and France.

the interests of all. Specifically, the great majority of the developing nations have signed the Nuclear Nonproliferation Treaty. Having thus renounced acquiring nuclear weapons for themselves, it was in their best interest to assure that their neighbors did not acquire them either. Yet most of them opposed this reform of the IAEA. Some explained that doing so would discriminate against them as developing nations, because the agency's proposed additional powers would be exercised in the developing countries. Others argued that the five nuclear powers should lose their exemptions first, and most agreed that the IAEA could not exercise the functions of a police force. The countries that were actually engaging in nuclear proliferation, such as India, Pakistan, and Iran were—of course—the most vocal in this regard. Since within the IAEA each country had one vote, the proposed reforms quickly died.

The debates lasted for six months and left all the participants with a real feeling of unease, because they showed only too well how national sensibilities could override the interests of collective security. A few industrialized countries even moved to replace the IAEA's Swedish director, who was less than courageous, but they gave up the attempt. In such a climate, he could easily have been replaced by the representative of a country that was working on a bomb!

The total powerlessness of the IAEA seems permanent. It considerably limits the length of the future life of the NPT, which was voted in May 1995. Without the signatures of the countries now in violation and without the tools for verification, this text will most likely remain more of a moral tract than an effective defense treaty. The same is true of the treaty prohibiting chemical weapons, until thirty-five countries sign it. By June 1995, two years after its initial signing, only twelve of the 120 signatory States had ratified that treaty.

The very structure of the international legal system prevents it from assuming a political role. It keeps adding on texts and ramifications without end. Today there are several dozen international agreements and thousands of specialized legal documents, not to mention those generated by the multilateral agencies whose numbers and members keep right on growing. There are also dozens of regional entities with similar ambitions and outputs of paper. But what all this adds up to is nothing but a complex and powerless Tower of Babel.

This system proceeds more by its own bureaucratic logic than by any political will: no common vision is guiding it. The only political impetus behind it is on the level of backing broad political principles that no one would dare dispute but that no one would be naive enough to try to apply, either. Administrative organizations and legal frameworks can multiply forever without any regulatory system developing that can actually promote order. And so it is that in the shadow of this mighty but futile formalism such soft laws are multiplying; they cover only subjects that they can name and discuss without actually affecting the reality of them. Codes, declarations, and other resolutions are all the rage, but they only commit those willing to follow them when they want to follow them.

Such soft laws find their counterparts in neutral political institutions, of which the nongovernmental organizations (NGOs) are typical. There are over five thousand of these.[9] It is a matter of creating "real-life laws"; this ambition in itself testifies to the lack of credibility and the inadequacy of the existing international legal structures.

The proliferation of these entities and of these poorly defined rights is vainly attempting to bridge the gap between the utopian law and the reality. The growth and spread of international law will not spontaneously create collective security, any more than economic integration could. These twin utopias share the same powerlessness because they are both founded upon the same error: they fail to take into consideration the States themselves.

CHAPTER 7

Law Against Peace?

One must be careful not to judge newborn societies with
the ideas of those that no longer exist.

—Alexis de Tocqueville, *Reflexion sur la révolution*

The Dangerous Multiplication of States

For many years international law was the most faithful ally of the
States. For at least the last three centuries, it has been the only
force legitimizing their representation of the nations. As early as
1648, the Treaty of Westphalia, which ended the Thirty Years'
War, enshrined the equality and the sovereignty of States as the
foundations of the international order. But the development of the
utopian law has broken up this venerable alliance. For the importance assumed by the law nowadays makes it imperative for nations to acquire the mantle of Statehood—at the risk of
cheapening it. There were 44 recognized States in 1850, 51 in
1903, 60 in 1938, 108 in 1963, 144 in 1983, and 191 in 1995.
The number of States has therefore more than tripled since 1940.
The utopian law makes this trend inevitable; not to be a State
means not to exist. Without official recognition as a State, no
money, no security, no sovereignty, not even a voice. Conversely,
the club of States gives the highest consideration to even the tiniest
of its members. Many international conferences have been stalled
by the unexpected opposition of one of these small States, whose
population and GNP are smaller than those of the French city of

Lyons. It took a whole night in 1992 to overcome Malta's opposition to the CSCE's declaration on Yugoslavia. The forty-nine other states present, including the United States, Russia, and the twelve European Union members, labored patiently to overcome this hurdle. Another time, it was Cyprus that had an independent opinion on the major disarmament treaties. For several days, both the NATO and the Warsaw Pact countries played the game of pretending to listen to Cyprus.

This utopian generalization of a model conceived by and for the great States of history is dangerous. It is a powerful incentive to political fragmentation. Today any population with a sense of its collective identity constitutes itself a State—it has no other choice if it wants to be taken seriously. The absolute legitimacy of Statehood is the only clear political message of the international legal system. But this external recognition of States often has no connection with their internal legitimacy. These States exist more by virtue of the recognition they receive from outside than because they actually represent a nation in an organized way.

The increase in the number of States in the past ten years represents a very distinct phenomenon, quite different from what we saw in the 1950s. During the postcolonial period, the point was to give the world's geography a certain political plausibility. Then, beginning in the 1970s, the fragmentation process began to speed up.

Twenty-one new States appeared between 1971 and 1984, most of which are small in size. Since 1985, twenty-four more have been created; conditions in them are usually mediocre. Twenty-six of the forty-five countries created in the past 25 years are "extremely poor" according to the World Bank's criteria. To take only one example, the per capita GNP of the eight Asian States of the former USSR was $600 in 1992, that is to say comparable to conditions in Yemen, Honduras, or Zimbabwe. Because most of these States have been ravaged by war, factoring in their subsistence economies (not included in GNP calculations) does not improve the picture.

As to the three Baltic States, their $800 per capita GNP places them at the same level as Cuba or Bolivia. Even if we double this figure to take barter into account, they are still far behind Bulgaria, as well as such countries as Mauritius and Costa Rica. Today, half the countries in the world have a population under 7,000,000 (the size of Switzerland) and a GNP of $10 billion (the same figure as the total economy of Luxembourg—or the added value of Renault,* which ranks only 150th among the world's corporations). This fragmentation of sovereignties has significantly increased in the past twenty years: thirty-five of the forty-five States created since 1970 have fewer than 6,000,000 inhabitants. These figures are a clear indication of the fragmentation that the multiplication of States has produced.

The Utopian Law Is Undermining the States

Compared to the overvalued status of the State itself, the protections offered to individuals and minorities seem modest. The legal contrast is remarkable. The sovereignty of States derives from the most solemn legal documents in the system of international law. This is almost a tautology, since sovereignty is the bedrock of this very system. By contrast, the rights of individuals are guaranteed only by arrangements that are numerous but not very binding. These are the domain par excellence of soft laws, that is to say documents without any teeth: resolutions, declarations, and other statements of intent. They are not completely worthless or useless, but their scope and the protection they provide are limited. This limitedness is neither an insufficiency nor an accident; it is the logical consequence of the absolute primacy of States and of State sovereignty. To give individual human rights the same level of legal protections as States' rights would create endless problems that

---

*The added value of a company is its total sales less its total cost of production, excluding nonproduction costs. [Translator's note]

would undermine the primacy of States. States are encouraged to respect the general indications sketched out by the soft laws, but they actually do so only on their own sovereign terms. This difference in status between the individual and the State has considerable practical consequences.

The leaders of minorities know that their constituencies will never have the power to impose their will or confront their opponents unless they acquire the status of a State. The Biafrans, the Kurds, the Muslims of Bosnia, and others have measured the size of this difference with their blood. In such conditions, every minority group inevitably wants to form itself into a nation and then be recognized as a State.

Thus the utopian law ends up by destabilizing States. It wants to promote without delay the primacy of individual human rights. However, the only legal entities it recognizes are sovereign States. As a result, it encourages the multiplication of States, even if recognizing them will destabilize existing States rather than strengthen them. This quick-fix solution will cause many problems in the future. The divorce of the Czechs and the Slovaks is a good example. The Slovaks convinced themselves that they would never really exist as a people, at home or abroad, until they were officially recognized as a separate sovereign State. This was a constant theme in the conversations of Slovak leaders. When they were queried about the appropriateness of this decision, they all said they saw this as a first step towards forming a federation with the Czechs, but one that would be equitable this time around because both parties would be States. This prospect is distant at best, because the Czechs have no desire to form a federation with the Slovaks. Here as elsewhere, the reality is the fragmenting of populations into inward-looking groups, whose anxieties see protective magic in setting themselves up as a State.

Such artificial creations have only their legal status in common with the great States of history, which developed in a quite opposite way. Conscious of their limitations, especially their economic limitations, traditional States are committing themselves to forming strong regional groups. Some are considering collectively surrendering their sovereignty in order to become politically stronger as a group, and some are already committed to doing this. States that have come into being as the result of fragmentation, on the other hand, are above all the jealous guardians of an identity that is still in the process of establishing itself. Born of separation, they can hardly envisage uniting with their neighbors; indeed, latent antagonisms continue to flare up between them. We shall not see a three-State Baltic Federation any time soon—or, for that matter, a State of Southern Slavs or a West African confederation.

By encouraging this cancerous proliferation of States, the utopian laws irreparably weaken the very order that they would wish to create. Its goal is to create a society of States united by the shared values of democracy, human rights, and free trade. The reality is that it creates the exact opposite. The multiplication of States fragments not only territories and populations but these mighty principles themselves. This is because although the international legal system can confer sovereignty upon a State, it can never in and of itself legitimize that State's existence. And the majority of these States are born from the need of a minority to see its distinctness officially recognized. Thus they tend to cultivate their uniqueness. And the more the system attempts to impose one general-purpose model, the more the States, concerned to support their legitimacy against the claims of nations, emphasize their unique characteristics as States.

Universal Values Are Becoming Less and Less So

The spread of democracy in recent years has been accompanied by increasingly divergent interpretations, each convinced of its own legitimacy. The Polish and Czech democracies, for example, are without a doubt close to a Western "model," but they differ greatly from the Slovak or Romanian democracies—not to mention the democracy of Russia. Within the three Baltic countries, the idea of democracy is not the same in Vilnius as it is in Tallinn; the large Russian minorities there know all about that. The democracy of Kirghizia would not seem alien to us. The democracy of Kazakhstan has more in common with the enlightened paternalism of Egypt or Singapore than it has with English parliamentarianism. The democratic systems of Japan and Taiwan are idiosyncratic and restrictive, while those of the Philippines and India have strong European roots.[88,75] Mexico's "institutional" democracy—with its de facto poll tax—more closely resembles that of Malaysia than that of the United States. Buoyed by their economic success, many Asian countries defend the specifically Asian and often restrictive nature of their regimes, both as to their democracy and as to human rights issues.[105]

It would be dangerous to claim that these differences are exclusively a kind of local color. The idea that history will come to an end with economic and legal integration is really silly. Several things argue against it. First, there is the difference that separates such an integration from a true political order. Then there is the fact that this pressure to standardize is being resisted by many nations. The 1992 CSCE conference on the "human dimension," held in Moscow, revealed profound differences among the countries of Europe regarding human rights and their political applications. This despite the fact that these countries adhere to the same principles and belong to the same institutions that are supposed to embody them and safeguard them. A year later, the major United Nations conference in Vienna discovered even greater discrepancies with the Asian democracies.

Voluntarist, centralized, and unified States such as France or Spain cannot share the same concepts of equality and citizenship as pluralist and decentralized States such as Hungary or India. The former States are convinced that only a single common status for all citizens can guarantee civil peace by guaranteeing liberty for everybody. The latter States are convinced that the only way to achieve this is to scrupulously recognize the rights of each of their minorities. Both schools are convinced that history is on their side. Cultures where identity and responsibility are seen as collective, such as Japan or China, cannot have the same conception of the rights of the individual as cultures such as those of the United States or Scandinavia, where identity and responsibility are viewed as belonging to the individual. Such differences permeate daily life.

In the corporations of the English-speaking countries, for example, precise job descriptions lay out the responsibilities and level of information of every employee. No such thing exists in Japan, where responsibility rests with an entire group of people. A central administrative director has a desk in the midst of the desks of his twenty colleagues and he holds his most important meetings right in front of all of them. In a Japanese business, managers are responsible for the actions of *all* of their subordinates. In 1990 a stockbroker employed in the New York branch of a Japanese bank lost $40 million in one day, more than the monthly profit of the bank's entire American operation. The bad decision was his, but the huge consequences of his actions also resulted from his superior not properly defining his decision-making powers. The stockbroker was demoted but not dismissed; his superior, however, was fired. In an even more surprising move, the head of the bank's American operation was sanctioned and recalled to Tokyo, where the Director of International Business was transferred and the bank's entire board of directors lost their quarterly bonuses. The Japanese system encourages collective responsibility just as naturally as the American system discourages it. These differences do not prevent all the parties involved from formally embracing the same legal principles, but each culture reads them and applies them in a very different way.

What is true of political principles also holds for economic ones.

Economic forces, because they are so strong, always have a double-edged relationship with States. Of the 200 States in the world, only thirty have GNP's greater than those of the world's largest corporations. This comparison is even more telling if one considers that most corporations concentrate this wealth in only a few of their activities. The computer R&D expenses of IBM are higher than those of any country in the world except the United States and Japan. The economic weakness and small size of most States, relative to large private corporations or the movements of capital, make them unable to control their own economic situation. This forced internationalization of their economies places most young or fragile States in untenable positions. They are drawn, or rather pulled, toward external integration and enforced modernization. These tensions undermine their domestic legitimacy, and widen the gap between recently created, weak States and stronger societies with completely different backgrounds and tempos.

This discrepancy can be seen in even the most advanced countries, such as those of the European Union. Take for instance the hunters of southwestern France, who have been deprived of their favorite sport by European Community regulations that protect wild birds, or the fishermen of Spain, who feel shut out by the EU's drive to increase agricultural production. These resentments exist even when the advantages of integration are obvious to the countries in question; it would be imprudent to view these feelings as nothing more than nostalgia for a simpler past.

These resentments are even harsher in less developed countries, where international integration is felt to be not advantageous but a source of problems. The elimination of subsidies for essential goods, the closing of money-losing corporations, or the opening of a country's borders to imports that compete unfairly with local producers—perhaps these changes will bring economic benefits to such countries eventually, but in the meantime their people can't eat economic forecasts.

To assume that free trade and the market economy are natural and thus universal is a dangerous mixture of naïveté and ignorance. A glance at economic history shows that our free economies are the product of very slow and very complex processes. The difficulties that Eastern Europe is experiencing in developing such economies is but one indication. In spite of strong consumer demand, pretty good credit, and fair production capacity, these countries have had trouble putting these together effectively in the marketplace. They understand that this entails reforming not only their organizations and regulations but also their habits and behavior patterns. But even once it has been established, a market economy can be viewed in very different, even contradictory ways, depending on whether one is in Tokyo or Washington, Paris or London. These conflicts concern more than tactics; often they reflect real cultural differences.

In the 1980s, for example, the United States accused Japan of systematically dumping computer chips. Faced with the inexorable increase in Japan's percentage of the world market, which leaped from 15 percent to 50 percent in ten years, the United States insisted on pricing agreements. In order to calculate these, they forced Japanese companies to open their accounting records to the American government, which was convinced that it could find irrefutable proof of Japan's bad faith. It became clear, however, that in Japanese firms most costs were fixed costs, including both their equipment and their personnel, who were never fired. Their selling prices, then, reflected only variable costs—which in the case of chips were rather low: nothing but energy, a few chemical products, and silicon. The Japanese producers could therefore logically set very low prices, which would have been impossible had they used different budgeting principles. As for free trade, the violence and the recurrence of the business conflicts within GATT have reminded everyone that free trade is not a natural phenomenon and that establishing and maintaining it requires both vigilance and a certain amount of conflict.

The Legitimacy of States Is the
Key Issue in International Relations

As they develop, legal and economic integration force States to submit increasingly to rules made outside their borders. Few States are powerful enough to have any control over the making of these rules. This distances States from nations, whose defining characteristics are brushed off or ignored in favor of such universals as human rights, democracy, or free trade. These debates affect even the most powerful States, as evidenced by the fierce debates in Canada and the United States over NAFTA, and in Europe over the Maastricht Treaty. For all parties involved, the main issue is the same: how legitimate is the institution of the State?

When the European Union was ratified, a question arose in Europe that is normally heard only in countries in disarray: how legitimate is the power that represents the nation? This concern became all-out anxiety among the smaller nations of the European Union, in spite of the fact that the EU assures them a remarkable degree of political and statutory equality. Nevertheless, these countries are fearful of being swallowed up in a rigid system where they will have little power. They fear being subjected to imperatives that will ignore them because those imperatives reflect the will of the larger countries. For these smaller countries, the transformation of economic power into political power represents an existential threat.

In these old European countries, long plagued by wars, then brought together by a half-century of peaceful coexistence, we now see the same fissures as in the troubled South. Just as the modernized elites of the countries of the South often support radical opposition movements, otherwise moderate European elites now support opposition to a political European Union. They accuse the Union of being a voluntarist, abstract, and arbitrary construction, put together by a few leaders with a complete disregard for the instinct of nations. This debate is indeed a crisis of legitimacy, that is to say it is about the embodiment by the States of the identity and the self-awareness of nations.

This crisis is new in its depth and in its scope. In the vast majority of countries today, States are having an increasingly hard time reconciling their integration into the international system with their domestic obligations, which consist of assuring the representation of the nation and making sense of its social and economic development. These difficulties represent a weakening of the State's authority, but always on the level of politics. The more the State integrates itself into the international system and insists, "Let's join the others," the more the nation grows uneasy and begins to ask itself, "Who are we?"

Some countries reject regulation by the International Monetary Fund because they feel that such regulation does not sufficiently take into account any one country's uniqueness. For the same sickness the same cure—and never mind who the patient is. This disregard of national cultures in favor of general rules will eventually turn the utopian dream of integration into a nightmare. And the States that accept these procedures risk weakening their own legitimacy. This is as true for the United Kingdom or Denmark as it is for Peru or Kenya. To be convinced of this, we have only to read the many addenda that the leaders of certain countries insisted on including in the 1993 Maastricht Treaty. The Danes, for example, opposed the unregulated purchase of a second home in Denmark by citizens of other European Community countries. The matter may appear trivial compared to the vast stakes of the Treaty, even contradictory to its spirit. But such a contrast shows how wide the gulf is between the desire of States to integrate and the desire of nations to preserve their identity. Reconciling the two is the key to the future survival of States.

In fact, once the legitimacy of the State is questioned there is a strong risk that the nation will break down into many smaller communities.

Social archaisms become powerfully legitimate once again: they embody the community's fight to preserve itself against the threat of an aggressive and alien modernism. States then use these same mechanisms to restore their own legitimacy. They thus commit themselves to a dangerous balancing act. Externally they must defend their image as a modern State that favors integration: they join all the political-legal clubs that prove this policy. Domestically, however, they favor conservative forces, with the goal of stabilizing their populations and easing their transitions. But this balancing act never holds up, because the forces at play are too strong to be successfully manipulated. These forces can be controlled only by a legitimate State, that is, one governed by a majority.

The rise in ethnic, religious, or nationalist demands does not spring from the agenda of a political opposition, but rather from the inadequacy or the illegitimacy of the agenda of the State. Only legitimacy itself can bridge the gap between the State and its nations, between external integration and domestic order. This is an essential factor in a country's defense, even for the most developed countries. The whole purpose or task of State legitimacy is to answer the question of national identity. If this issue is not resolved, States find themselves torn apart by demands that they cannot meet: on one hand they try their best to modernize their countries and to integrate them into systems whose norms are completely alien; on the other hand they try to make their citizens comply with these changes, which have not made their daily lives any better or given them any more protection than before.

The Illegitimacy of the State, the Main Source of Instabilities

This misalignment between the domestic and external domains, between the State as country and the State as citizenry, can happen in any country, rich or poor, democratic or authoritarian. The consequences for such a country's security are enormous. The insufficient legitimacy of States is the main cause of instabilities, whether domestic or international—the former most often causing the latter.

The first consequences of this insufficiency are naturally felt at home. Legitimacy is a zero-sum game: "counter-powers" win only what is given up to them by the weakening of States. Whether they are paramilitary bandits or religious fundamentalists, these counter-powers are not controlled by occult forces. The public's taste for the sensational and for conspiracy theories encourages such misinterpretations and diverts our attention from the really meaningful political question. Wherever one looks it is the weakening of the State that creates new openings, for example, for illicit traffics—and traffickers. They can only ply their trade in whatever space they can grab—or, more often, that is abandoned to them. That is the conclusion of those who have spent their lives combating such things.

It is startling to hear an American colonel, a specialist in fighting drug dealers, conclude that in his experience "[D]rug dealers will never be beaten as long as they symbolize a simple and immediate form of social justice, economic equity, and minimum prosperity for all . . . The armed struggle against drug traffickers will never end as long as they remain more legitimate than the State in the eyes of the poor."[93] The drug traffic is a famous example of a counter-power because of its consequences in the West, but the importance of legitimacy is the same everywhere. The defeat of France in Algeria and of the United States in Vietnam and in the drug war in South America all come back to this very simple question of legitimacy.

The weakness of the State is the primary and the usual cause of instabilities, because it shows that the State is withdrawing from its nations. This is a physical reality. When entire urban neighborhoods or rural districts completely elude any kind of public order except the criminal kind (gangs, death squads, and the like), when none of the most basic public services (such as clean drinking water) are provided, the State simply ceases to exist in the eyes of the people and of course loses all legitimacy for them. By disappearing, the State opens the door to all sorts of counter-powers, which mix criminal activities with political demands.

In Southeast Asia, Burmese generals sell heroin across the border in China in order to buy weapons, using the excuse that their junta has been cut off from the world economy. Their Thai colleagues deposed the president of Thailand in 1991 on grounds of corruption. The problem was not that he was diverting public funds, but that he had broken up the finely calibrated sharing out of drug profits among his country's military leaders. In China, the police and the customs officials are quite busy these days. In 1992, they appropriated all the shares in one of the major privatized corporations in Shenzhen. In 1993, when the Hong Kong police caught several of them red-handed selling stolen cars, the Chinese border police took their Hong Kong counterparts hostage! The Pakistani security forces are financing "their" war in Afghanistan with the sale of heroin, which has reached 5 percent of Pakistan's GNP. This enormous sum of money is destabilizing both the border region and Pakistan itself. There were no heroin addicts in Pakistan in 1980; today there are two million. . . .[33]

In the Middle East, the Syrian army in Lebanon closely supervises the Bekaa Valley. The valley is a strategic axis; more important, the Syrian military supervises its poppy fields, which serve to supplement the retirement funds of its officers and the pay of its troops.

In South America, from the Amazon to the mountains of Colombia and Peru, security forces are often found to be intimately involved in the traffic that they are supposed to be interdicting. The most extreme case is undoubtedly that of Bolivia. In 1985, Bolivia experienced its 189th coup d'état in 120 years. It was organized—for the modest price of $1.3 million—by Roberto Gómez, the most powerful cocaine kingpin in the country, who then put into power one of his underlings, General Meza. Meza—

and this was the whole purpose of the coup—then named Gómez's brother minister of the interior and of police. This assured Roberto of peace and quiet in the family business, which soon bloomed spectacularly.

Other examples are legion; by their sheer numbers they become almost ordinary. Most often the entire State apparatus, in its most sensitive functions and up to the highest levels of the government, turns out to be not just corrupt but bought and paid for. In Argentina, the extent of the secret police's penetration into the public economy—in quest of booty rather than information—was one of the biggest problems that Raúl Alfonsín faced in the first years of his post-dictatorship reforms. The same problem permeates Eastern Europe. The economy has been taken over by the former secret police in Poland, Hungary, and Russia. Their leaders have established a corrupt but often effective business environment, which certain Americans view indulgently.[57] In Mexico, the corruption created by the principal cocaine-traffic networks reached such proportions that President Salinas had to officially denounce what was virtually a parallel government in a country already known for accommodating alternative interpretations of the law.

Once they have taken hold, these counter-systems become self-perpetuating. The ensuing empoverishment of the country and of some concerned parties makes them even more marginal and strengthens the position of these counter-powers. In Colombia, for example, the World Bank and the Inter-American Development Bank estimate that criminality has cost the country half of its possible growth over the past ten years.[93] This extra growth would have meant increasing by half the wealth of the average Colombian citizen. For most Colombians, this would have meant a substantial increase in their standard of living and a decreased attraction to crime. Such situations are not the property of underdeveloped countries alone. The United States offers an example of a developed country where this process is well under way. The marginalization of the black population has reached a level that makes any hope of its reversal unlikely. Today there are more young African-Americans in prison than in college. During the 1980s, two out of three African-Americans were born into fatherless households and half were born into acute poverty. What chance do children who are born into such circumstances have of ever finding their place in society?

This criminality is only one consequence out of many of the illegitimacy of the State in matters of security. Religious fundamentalism and nationalist movements make their inroads in exactly the same way; from this standpoint they are not different. In any case, we are just dealing with a redistribution of the responsibilities abandoned by the State. This is what is happening today in Algeria.

The Algerian State resolved to be a modern one. In foreign policy, it plugged into the system of international integration. Domestically, it dismantled its traditional religious and social structures. By attempting to totally renovate its society, the Algerian government condemned itself to needing total success. Not only did it fail, but a runaway population increase (50 percent of all Algerians are under twenty-five years old) means that most Algerians have no memory of or interest in the adventure that was the liberation of Algeria from French colonial rule. They see no future for themselves but chronic unemployment. In order to regain its lost legitimacy, the Algerian State has begun to play on the basic elements of the nation's identity: its language and its religion. It has imposed a nationalistic Arabization on its citizens. It has brought religious preachers from Egypt to replace the native-born Muslim academics, who have disappeared along with the traditional system of religious education. The new preachers chosen by the State were all fundamentalists. The government made this choice deliberately in order to revive the population's desire for religion. But the legitimacy that the government wanted to regain quickly slipped through its fingers. Because it was unable to answer this newfound nationalistic support with a credible economic and social policy the government lost whatever gains it had made, and the new religious movement that it had encouraged grew in power instead. Thus a new legitimacy has been created—nationalistic and religious—stemming from the State's illegitimacy rather than from any real political planning.

The development of mosques is an example of this phenomenon. In theory, the State takes responsibility for building them and for supplying them with imams* who agree with the government's policies. But because of chaos and delays on the construction sites, improvised mosques have popped up all over the place, more as social centers for the young than as places of worship. They have become that, of course, headed by local imams who are aware of the social realities, close to the people, and considered legitimate because they live among them. The spread of fundamentalist Islam in Algeria is not the result of an intransigent religiosity, as it is in Iran. The Islamic Salvation Front or FIS has taken hold in Algeria because of the opportunities that it offers to a directionless population to take their future back into their own hands. Fundamentalism also enjoys some support among women, in spite of a certain severity toward them. This is because the militant modernization of the State has brought Algerian women very little. Worse yet, in its attempts to re-Islamicize Algeria, the movement retained only the most backward aspects of the Koran in the form of a misogynistic civil code. The neighborhood imams, on the other hand, give women more consideration, a role to play, basically a status in the society. The failure of religious fundamentalism among the working classes, however, confirms that the success of the FIS results from the failure of the State rather than from its own merits:

*Highly respected laymen who read the Koran at services [Translator's note] it has not taken hold among the few social classes that have actually been helped by the actions of the State.

In Turkey, Islam, although officially banned as a State religion, is growing in strength through similar mechanisms: social services and a stabilizing presence in areas abandoned by the government. In the last municipal elections, Islamic parties received 40 percent of the vote in the working-class suburbs and won the general elections of 1996. A restaurant owner in one suburb explained this success with amazing accuracy: "A government that doesn't take care of the people isn't a government at all." An old Marxist union member, now a convert, added: "The law must come from God, otherwise politicians use it only for their own profit."

Farther away, China is undergoing a surprisingly similar experience. Travelers returning from the interior have all noted the amazing revival and growth of religious practices in China.[107] Popular traditions have been the first to make a comeback: village cults of ancestors and local divinities, rebuilding of Taoist temples, massive processions, celebrations, and family rituals . . . The State has not discouraged this resurgence because it hopes that it will help to stabilize the countryside. While it combats the opium of the poppy, it encourages the opium of religion: the Chinese government is aware of the increasing conflicts that the growing differences in wealth between the big cities and the rural areas could bring about. But it has gone further: it has tolerated the resurgence of imported religions, whether Christian or Muslim. In China today, there are 25,000 mosques, 600 Protestant churches and 300 Catholic churches. These are served by 20,000 imams, 6,000 Protestant ministers and 3,400 Catholic priests.[86] The idea, here too, is to show that the government, which has permitted a growing prosperity, is also open politically: it will oppose only those who seek to destroy it, such as the demonstrators at Tienanmen Square. Authorized and officially sanctioned, religions seem acceptable to the

Chinese government, but it combats those that are under "foreign influence." The independent Islam of the non-Chinese minorities, especially in the western part of China, is repressed. On the other hand the Islam of the Huei, who enjoy the status of a full-fledged minority, is encouraged. The important support that Huei Islam receives from Saudi Arabia is not a problem, since the Chinese and the Saudis have a close military and political relationship. The official Chinese "patriotic" Catholic Church, which accepts a hierarchy imposed by Beijing, is allowed, whereas the Roman Church is persecuted. Chinese Buddhism is welcome, whereas its Tibetan counterpart is outlawed as supporting an intolerable independence movement. But these subtle distinctions are becoming less and less important. As in Algeria, the reestablishment of even the most minimal religious infrastructure, initially encouraged by a State trying to gain legitimacy, has served as a starting point for a movement that that State can no longer control.

The Chinese situation shows that even the legitimacy conferred by real economic success is not enough. Political legitimacy is also needed. And Beijing sees a growing risk that a rival legitimacy may develop. Proselytizing by those religious groups could well contribute to this. The evolution in this direction of similar movements in Russia can only increase the fears of the Chinese authorities, who have begun to energetically suppress domestic churches, that is to say the unofficial religious communities whose numbers keep multiplying, and the religions with nationalistic overtones of Sinkiang or of Tibet. The strength of the State's social control in China and its economic success give it a freedom of action that does not exist in Africa, Central Asia, or Russia. For the time being, the desire for personal comfort is the number one preoccupation of the Chinese people and takes priority over any other concerns. Yet the danger persists. It could become a brutal reality if the government were to weaken or its economic growth slacken off. China's example pays eloquent testimony to the fact that a strong sovereign State and successful economic integration are not enough to overcome the risks of serious instability posed by the lack of legitimacy of the State.

The Lack of State Legitimacy
Draws Elites to Radical Oppositions

The weakening of the legitimacy of a State affects more than a country's most socially or geographically backward elements. Its consequences are certainly more visible in these areas, since entire zones or populations elude official authority and fall under the control of counter-powers. While less spectacular, its effects are even more serious on the scientific and technical elites. Being symbols of modernization, the members of these groups willingly identify themselves with their country's future. They are pampered by modernizing governments and eager to show off their progress. Governments expect these respected personalities to uphold to the public the official policy of international economic integration.

In fact, a large proportion of these elites often leave their own countries and have received their academic training abroad. Half of the students in the United States studying for masters' degrees in the hard sciences and in technology are foreigners.[96] The first study of this matter in France, started in 1991, also revealed that many doctoral programs were filled almost exclusively with foreign students or researchers. The same thing is true in most large industrial countries. These elites receive a broad exposure to world society. They seem to embody the agenda of international integration that their governments are so actively pursuing. These elites, therefore, should feel little attraction to nationalistic or religious movements. Yet in many cases the elites support these movements as soon as they receive strong popular legitimacy.

In Turkey during the 1970s a quarter of the representatives of the nationalist movement were qualified as engineers. In Iran, two of the principal ministers received their university degrees at American universities. In Algeria, the spokesman for the FIS or Islamic Salvation Front is a petroleum engineer. In Morocco, the head of the Islamic movement has a teaching degree in physics. And so on.

The voluntarist and reconstructionist rhetoric of these opposition movements attracts these elites, who refuse to resign themselves and want to take the future of their countries into their own hands. They tend to view their country's weakness as the result of its submission to the international system, which their nation's leaders have accepted. It is incredibly humiliating, for example, for an Indian or a Brazilian engineer to see his country forbidden to buy or sell certain technologies by a club of countries more highly developed than his own. His resentment, directed towards his own government and the outside world, comes from both his political beliefs and his personal situation.

The living conditions of such a professional are often mediocre. Egypt, for example, qualifies 3,000 engineers a year. Half of these are unemployed, in spite of the country's tremendous need for modernization. Egypt has one physician for every 800 people, that is to say as many as France in the 1960s. Most cannot live solely from their fees, even though the health-care needs of Egypt are great. Underemployed, underpaid, and often forced to take unpleasant second jobs, the elite bitterly resent this waste of human resources. For them it comes to symbolize the problems of their countries, where the businessmen and the politicians control all the resources for their own profit alone.

These are the main reasons for the success of the Algerian FIS among the technical elites that have remained in that country. They have embraced their government's rhetoric about modernity, but they realize that all sorts of corruption and compromises have rendered that government powerless. The rhetoric of the FIS revives their desire for development. The FIS is well received when it declares that technical modernization is essential if Algeria is to take its destiny into its own hands and that it will make this a priority when it comes to power. In most of the Arab countries, the social base of Islamic fundamentalism is not a powerful, fanatical clergy but disempowered elites. In large part, the popularity of fundamentalism is the result of a mismanaged modernization campaign during which the State has lost its legitimacy. An analysis by the Egyptian police of the profile of arrested fundamentalists is revealing: 35 percent are university undergraduates, 10 percent are graduates, and 5 percent are high-school students—in other words, half of them are well educated.

These elites blame the State not for its desire to integrate into the international system but the submissive way it goes about it. They reject the idea that a handful of world powers should impose their demands on their country, instead of their country putting forth its own identity and interests. This open nationalism, advocated by many of these elites, is often a far cry from the wary, even xenophobic nationalism of many of the movements that they nevertheless end up supporting. These converging contradictions are particularly obvious in India.

This country offers the rather astonishing example of an absolutely dominant religion—Hinduism—which feels threatened by the other religions of India, in spite of the fact that 80 percent of all Indians are Hindu. Since 1925, fundamentalist Hinduism has tried to prove that its religious community constitutes a nation, as much for cultural reasons as because of blood ties. In the manner of all nationalist movements, it has rewritten India's history to make it Hindu. This has not been well accepted. The social separations of the caste system were sacred and therefore could not be debated; this prevented the development of a political advocacy of national unity. In addition, the Indian elites were saturated with Marxism and the transition from colonialism was successful. It produced a better standard of living for most people and protected India's democratic institutions, allowing them to continue to function.

Hindu fundamentalism became successful when the technical elites started to feel that India was fragile and possibly in decline. Increasing disorders—linked to religious conflicts, the West's support of Pakistan because of its role as a rear-area base in the Afghan war, the economic emergence of China, and the collapse of its Soviet ally—all caused India's elites to fear that their country's future was in grave danger. Since the mid 1980s, this decline has always been the central theme of the speeches of the Hindu fundamentalist movement and its banner-carrying party, the Bharatiya Janata Party (BJP). The BJP has relegated historical considerations to the background in favor of a rhetoric very much like the ideology of national security of a Latin American dictator.

The BJP emerged from its ideological and religious ghetto to embrace the cause of Indian power. By so doing, it began to attract the country's elites to its ranks. It continues to lay siege to a government that is trying to juggle having to support this nationalistic rhetoric on the one hand, while concerned to appease domestic conflicts and needing to maintain good relations with the West. In each case, the government has been forced to make decisions that the BJP has denounced as weakening India: making concessions to Muslims, accepting humiliating political and economic constraints imposed by other countries, etc. For example, when applying international regulations limiting dangerous exports, India turns out to be forbidden to buy or sell certain technologies. The BJP and the elites unanimously denounce the government's submissiveness. On the other hand, if the Indian government decides to bypass these regulations and is accordingly sanctioned by the international community, then it is India that is humiliated; this can only result from the weakness of the State.

That happened twice in 1992. India wanted to buy from Russia ballistic technologies whose sale is forbidden by the international regulations that control such exports. Russia is not a member of this international agreement but claims to adhere to it. The United States has successfully exerted tremendous pressure on Russia to respect this commitment, and its efforts have been successful. Later, India was accused of shipping to Iran a cargo of certain chemicals whose sale is prohibited because of their possible military uses. A

United States-led initiative pressured India into proving its good faith by allowing the ship in question to be inspected. The ship was tracked from anchorage to anchorage, and the matter snowballed until India finally gave in. India was once again publicly humiliated by the forcible application to it of a regulation that it had never endorsed.

To defend themselves against the seductive powers of the radical opposition parties, States are tempted to shore up their legitimacy by adopting as their own the most crowd-pleasing projects of the opposition forces. They invariably lose at this game, but this only becomes clear with time, when the weakness of the State can no longer be compensated by the system in power. It took Algeria ten years and Pakistan fifteen to understand the consequences of their policies of Islamicization with no real social and economic modernization. Because States are supposed to be decisive and to act, they are always caught out by their contradictions and discredited still further. In the end, the radical opposition parties are the only beneficiaries of this. Politically irresponsible, rooted in social groups that are strangers to one another, they can preach both sides of any issue without risk. Both the BJP and the FIS are actually close to their country's power elites; but outside the developed urban areas, they have developed uncompromisingly religious platforms and a very isolationist view of relations with the outside world. This both-sides-of-the-mouth duplicity is particularly striking in a country like India, which is truly divided between an urban and economic elite (approximately 10 percent of the population), which holds the core of the country's wealth and power, and a poor rural mass. The BJP has a different speech for each group: nationalism and forward thinking for the rich, religion and xenophobia for the poor.

The solidarity of these oppositions is superficial. The Algerian FIS is actually an umbrella organization grouping together movements with very different clienteles and ideologies, which would make it extremely difficult for it to exercise official power. But the strength of these movements does not come from opposing one political organization to another. It comes from discrediting the State by directly addressing a question that the State will not address: the question of national identity. To answer the very basic questions, "What am I? Where do I belong? Who do I belong with?" these groups emphasize constituent elements of traditional identity that quickly gain spontaneous acceptance: religion, language, race, territory.

From the Utopia of Law to the Reality of War

These crises of the legitimacy of the State are really the identity crises of nations. They are the real world, far removed from the utopian constructs of economic and legal integration. These utopias eat away at the legitimacy of States, which alone can give meaning, and therefore stability, to nations.

This is so true that this same legal system encourages to the point of folly the multiplication of States, in order to give structure to collectivities in disarray. Finally, these utopias are very much impeded by the States. They dream of seeing them disappear and contribute to their weakening, but at the same time they don't know what to do without them, because in fact the international system continues to depend on their existence. How much longer will we able to continue to undermine this solitary pillar? The abstract status of "State" may well survive, but it risks ending up a mere shell with its real life, its legitimacy, emptied out of it. This is already the problem of all these phantom States created one after another by the utopian legal system. For these crises of the legitimacy of the State hold the key to future wars.

Utopian international law is an inexhaustible source of conflict because its order is that of sovereignty while its crises are crises of legitimacy. And nothing in this order links the one to the other.

In matters of security, the international order is based on the concept of sovereign States, that is to say countries that are able to assure their own integrity. It carefully codifies their power conflicts, but it fails to address the crises that arise out of their weakness. And these last are the most dangerous crises that the world has known to date. Such risks did not exist as long as the world was divided into a few dozen stable States. But this is no longer the case. Because of the weakness of many contemporary States, crises of legitimacy will less and less remain purely internal matters; they inevitably become international in nature. This broadening is not the result of some international plot, any more than the crises themselves are. The idea that vast international manipulations are orchestrated by drug lords or religious brotherhoods is wrong. It is a vision inherited from the Cold War and it is as out of date as the Cold War itself. Such an interpretation works for conflicts of sovereignty, where certain countries try to destabilize others in order to weaken and even control them. Today, the internationalization of crises of legitimacy is simply the natural result of the weakness of States.

It can result, for example, from the State's inability to control its most basic instruments of authority, such as the police, the army, or the secret services. Trafficking by the Thai military is contributing to the prolongation of the Cambodian crisis. In exchange for gemstones, the Thais offer the Khmer Rouge weapons and sanctuary. In China, the army directly manages arms exports with a liberalism that would place Milton Friedman or Jeffrey Sachs to the left of Karl Marx. It sells to anyone who can pay sophisticated weapons that other countries refuse to export. In South Asia, the Pakistani intelligence service, controlled by the Pashtoons, is waging a merciless war in Afghanistan to gain control of the opium trade. And so forth.

In other cases, internationalization results from the simultaneous weakening of States whose oppositions are similar in kind. It is tempting in such a case to reverse the order of cause and effect and to see in such a situation the workings of some vast plot. The best example is certainly the spread of Muslim fundamentalism. It would be easy but entirely wrong to see any orchestrated movement behind its varying manifestations. Close examination of the facts shows that the Islamic movements are actually weak on the international level. Their international commitments are entirely dominated by the interests of whichever countries they belong to.[102]

Thus during the Gulf War each such group's position was strictly aligned with that of its government. The best example is probably that of the Muslim Brethren. This movement originated in Egypt and has spread to most of the Arab countries. Its different branches maintain a point of contact in Egypt, but they lack any coordination or headquarters—as can be seen by the diversity of their local status. In Syria, the Brethren were crushed and forced into exile for having caused disruptions (the revolt of Hamas in 1982). In Jordan they are moderate and very close to the King. In Palestine they are extremists and opposed to the PLO, which they combat militarily. In Kuwait they are close to the center of power, but they are forbidden in Saudi Arabia. In Algeria, they oppose the FIS. And so on. Everywhere the actions of these movements turn out to be linked to the politics of the State, which supports them because they serve its interests.[102]

Political factors—nationality and power—are always stronger than religious factors. In Sudan a member of the Muslim Brethren leads the Darfur guerrillas against the government in Khartoum, whose allegiance is Arabic before it is Muslim. In Algeria, the Arabization policy of the FIS is above all anti-Berber. In Malaysia, the Islamic movement is even more anti-Chinese than it is pro-Muslim. In Afghanistan, the powerful Islamic student movement, which reconquered the country in a year, is manipulated by the Pakistani security service and is an instrument for imposing Pashtoon domination. And so forth.

On the other hand, in many Muslim countries the weakening of

State legitimacy has given rise to radical opposition groups that use religion as a pretext for their political aims. The result is that Islamic principles have penetrated into the organization of society. This is once again the result of the insufficient legitimacy of the State, which makes endless concessions because it is unable to impose its authority. It's not Islam that is spreading, it's the weakness of the State.

Elsewhere, internationalization is the result of the temptation of weak States to seek their salvation in radicalization. The logic of such States is that of a crusade in the name of a threatened identity. Iran is a perfect example: the political power there seems to be drifting towards a cult of martyrdom and an endlessly progressing radicalization. The Vatican of John Paul II is not far from a similar situation. In the face of widespread dissatisfaction within the Catholic Church, the Pope's trips are exercises in political leadership and recruiting campaigns: he is raising troops rather than elevating souls. John Paul II is turning out to be a remarkable war leader whose breviary seems to be Clausewitz and Kissinger. His priority is the strengthening of the institution of the Catholic Church. His goal is to (re)conquer all of the positions that have been surrendered by the personal torments of his predecessors and their misguided outreaches. He uses every opportunity, with a clear vision of this goal as his priority. The Church's indifference to peace in Yugoslavia as long as the Catholic States remained unrecognized was a remarkable example of this. In such a spirit, doctrine, not faith, is the priority. The defense of Church doctrine has become so obviously politicized that a bishop commenting on the last encyclical (bearing the revealing title "The Splendor of Truth") called it "more Roman than Catholic." When the Pope declares, "If God has called upon me with the ideas that I have, it means that they have a universal value," his logic is no different from that of the Ayatollah Khomeini. A missionary conviction dominates the thinking of both as they deal with the rapid erosion of their legitimacy, that is to say the interest and attention of their flocks.

Examples abound of the revival of crusades of every religion. Their religious bent does not confer any special character on these movements. The forces at work are the same that motivate all crises of legitimacy and transform them into more or less open international crises. What is being done in the name of religion can also be done in the name of race, language, or nationality. The Argentine military adventure in the Falklands, that of Iraq against Iran, or that of Peru against Ecuador provide recent examples.

The international order has no answer to these crises of legitimacy. As a result, the system is often accused of indifference or global irresponsibility towards people in favor of States. It becomes an accomplice in the eyes of those who feel abandoned or betrayed by this State into which they are being assimilated against their will. The system's response to this accusation is to give the complainants the opportunity to become full-blown, independent States. The utopian legal system thus aggravates the consequences of crises of legitimacy by giving them the means to expand. This opening can often seem like a peacemaking tool. In a way, this mirrors the institution of the amicable divorce. But amicable divorces are even rarer between nations than they are between married couples. From Korea to Bangladesh to Yugoslavia, recent history has shown us that separation into separate countries is generally very violent, and relations between the parties remain violent afterward. The States that are formed in this way are weak and have no claim to legitimacy other than an insistent affirmation of national identity.

In Central Asia, for example, the weakness of the States has led to the encouragement of an artificial and vengeful nationalism. These States thus hope to avoid the disintegration that could easily follow from the amazing confusion of that region.

Tadjikistan, for example, was separated from Uzbekistan only in

1929, but Uzbekistan kept the two largest historic cities: Samarkand and Bukhara. The borders separating the two countries are surrealistic: when he follows the Ferghana Valley westward—a perfectly straight line—the traveler leaves Uzbekistan, enters Tadjikistan, and re-enters Uzbekistan before finally arriving in Kirghizia.[103] The inhabitants have no notion whatsoever of nationality and are all bilingual. This situation poses no problems as long as their national governments are far away. If they want to affirm their existence, however, they must promote a militant nationalism.

Thus in Tashkent, the Uzbek capital, it is proved that the Tadjiks are really Uzbeks, and in Dushanbe, the Tadjik capital, it is proved that the Uzbeks are really Tadjiks. In reality neither of these statements is wrong. In Dushanbe it is said that the Uzbeks are all descendants of the Tadjiks and that they pretend to have forgotten how to speak Farsi. In Tashkent it is proved that the Tadjiks are Turkic speakers and that at least half are Uzbek in origin. For good measure, the Uzbeks have decided to invent a new language, derived from their nineteenth-century language and supplemented by a mixture of modern Arabic and Farsi. The result has been to plunge into confusion entire populations already ruined by war and mortally polluted by the byproducts of the monocultivation of cotton.

By contrast, their northern cousins, the Kazakhs and the Kirghiz, illustrate the successes that are possible for the legitimate State. Starting with an economic situation only slightly better than that of the Uzbeks and the Tadjiks, they played the game of institutional and economic modernization by adopting easy but symbolic measures that gained them both a little credit and a little time. They emphasized the value of citizenship in order to move beyond ethnic differences. They launched decentralization and privatization initiatives that gave individuals the impression that they were taking their affairs into their own hands. This improved the image of the State itself. Their ultimate success is not guaranteed, but their chances have much improved, and this only sharpens the contrast with the decline of their southern neighbors, of whom they have become increasingly wary. The cause of nationalism is already being lost.

That will only make it more dangerous as time goes on, because feelings of belonging have sprung up where historically there was no belonging. The Tadjiks, for example, did not exist as such in the nineteenth century: the Farsi-speaking city-dwellers were never called by this name, which was then used only for a few peasants living on certain mountains.[103] Similarly in Afghanistan we see the Pashtoons—who have never been a nation and today represent only 40 percent of Afghanistan's population—convince themselves over the years that the country belongs to them. The next step, one assumes, is ethnic cleansing, which they have already begun in eastern Afghanistan.

Such is the price of utopianism in lawmaking. The need for a formal geopolitical order results in States appearing in places where structured nations never existed, and those States try to construct nations in order to give themselves a minimum of reality. In doing so, however, they unleash nationalist passions that then lead them in directions that they had not anticipated.

It turns out that Tocqueville was right after all and on a grander scale than anticipated: what he thought necessary for a federated State is also true of any system of States. The increasing integration of States does not necessarily integrate their nations; the two can be completely separate, as in Southeast Asia, or opposed to each other, as in the examples just discussed.

This is the basic lesson to remember: the economic factors favoring integration may be powerful and active yet they do not necessarily favor political or social order. This truth was long hidden by security concerns and political slogans. The East–West confrontation imposed order and created artificial groupings, such as those of the Third World or the West. Without these masks, the difference between integration and order is now obvious. There is no alternative to restablishing the legitimacy of the State. The sovereignty of the

State means little in African States, where ethnic legitimacy prevails and justifies the massacres of Rwanda, Mauritania, Sudan, and Angola. It also means nothing in Yugoslavia or in Kashmir. By privileging the sovereignty of States with no concern for their legitimacy, the utopian system of international law is abandoning a growing number of nations between a rock and a hard place. On one side, a weak State that exists a little bit externally and scarcely at all internally; on the other, a bankrupt society incapable of organizing itself but whose conflicting groups share a common hostility to an outside world perceived as a threat. The international order is a real time bomb ready to explode: its rigidity and the powerful authority of its dogma lock countries into predicaments to which there is no peaceful solution.

CHAPTER 8

Wars of Necessity

Politics can be carried away by the tidal wave of military
necessity. As the unhappy countries draw closer and closer
to the abyss, the dreadful machinery begins to move and
little by little moves of itself.

—Winston Churchill, *The World Critics* (1923)

Has War Become Incomprehensible to Us?

In the five years that the utopian legal system has been in full
swing, it has not secured the peace or security of a single country,
nation, or minority. These five years of a new international order
have already got the deaths of over a million people on their charge
sheet. That's a high price to pay for any apprenticeship. Only the
prestige of the Superpowers has been able to resolve a few crises
and limit a few slaughters. As for the system itself, it operates with
an anxious indifference that talks about everything, acts on little,
and solves nothing. It pompously manages its impotence by loudly
proclaiming generous standards that it is unable to enforce. It is
undermined by the lack of legitimate States powerful enough to
guarantee their nations just representation of their existence and
their differences. The price of this ineffectuality is enormous. To
Ghassan Salamé's question "Who benefits from the breakdown of
States?" there is only one answer: "War." And war always has many
customers.

The proliferation of conflicts is inescapable and it has caught us short. We, the developed countries, are the only architects and the only beneficiaries of the international system as it now exists; we have ended up believing its rhetoric and good intentions, and seem genuinely surprised that others are not paying attention to them. What we have forgotten is that the only instrument of peace these last fifty years was the fear of mutual assured nuclear destruction. This certainty of death created the only truly imperative political rationality that ever existed. The disappearance of the logic of certain death immediately rendered the international political system void of all substance, but not of all usefulness. It continues to codify an order that is to our advantage, because its values and its principles are ours.

Every one of the countless documents put out by this system seems to consolidate this income of power by endorsing the validity of its principles. It is easy for us to convince ourselves then that a new international order is really being created—still in its infancy but coming along. The fact that we often admit this system's weakness actually reflects credit on it, somehow. In spite of himself, Bernard Kouchner* is actually one of the pillars of the system that he so much despises. He criticizes the system's lack of zeal or its unwieldy bureaucracy, but his freedom to leap into action allows us to dream of an order that would strengthen the weak, defend the oppressed, and hunt down tyrants. He goes about things like a latter-day Marat, who wanted to "establish an altar to Justice and Liberty in every village." How could one not agree to such beautiful principles? And who could argue against them without condemning himself?

This moral high ground appears to us to guarantee the validity of a system that seems, also, to benefit everyone's well-understood best

---

*Bernard Kouchner is the former head of the French nonprofit organization Médecins sans Frontières (Doctors Without Borders). A former minister of public health and then of foreign aid, he now heads a "Green" (environmentalist) French political party. [Translator's note]

interests. Today more than ever there is no prosperity without order. This is especially true for developed countries, whose globalized economies cannot tolerate threats to free trade. The Persian Gulf is the only part of the world for which the United States ever considered waging a limited war—including a nuclear one—against the USSR (in 1974) and the only region where it has conducted large-scale military operations since then (in 1991). But free trade is just as essential for developing nations, whose growth is increasingly linked to economic integration. And economic integration depends on order.

We have only to compare Africa and Southeast Asia. In 1965, they had the same per capita GNP; thirty years later Southeast Asia's is six times higher. Many factors have played a role in this, but the disorder in Africa is a disastrous weakness, as evidenced by the absence of investment and trade, which continues to marginalize the continent. A prestigious American consulting firm pointed this out strikingly several years ago. Several large food-products companies had joined together to ask the firm for a projection of African investment. After two years of analysis, the recommendation was to invest only in the production and sale of beer. The firms were surprised that such a costly study would recommend such a modest investment. The consultants explained that there were many other credit-worthy opportunities in Africa, but that only beer was profitable enough for investors to get more than their money back within two years. And two years, the study specified, is the maximum length of time that a prudent investor could expect stability to last in Africa.

This double warning of morals and economics makes the development of wars incomprehensible to us. We have grown so used to thinking of war as the very last resort that we can no longer think of it as an everyday affair. All the ferocious "little" wars with no obvious interests at stake seem to be the actions of madmen. What haven't we written about Saddam Hussein or Slobodan Milosevic?

Such a step backward seems inconceivable to us: we can only explain these events as the actions of a couple of dangerous lunatics, as does Dr. Bernard Kouchner, physician and humanitarian, who calls for their immediate removal.

Have We Forgotten War?
A Serious but Comfortable Amnesia

Such naïveté as Dr. Kouchner's is disarming. To believe in human progress to the point of ignoring reality is as dangerous as it is common. We still believe that the weird peace created by the threat of certain death was the harbinger of a truly peaceful world. What complete ignorance of both recent and long-past history!

Why should war, once a daily occurrence, suddenly be a stranger to us? Because 10 percent of humanity was able to avoid it on its own territory for two generations? The same Europe that we are now trumpeting as a model of pacifism has been built by wars, down to the last stone. In the sixteenth century Europe knew only ten years of peace, in the seventeenth century only four, and in the eighteenth century sixteen. From 1500 to 1800, Europe was at war 270 years out of 300, with a new war every three years. Austria and Sweden—models of pacifism—were also at war every three years during these three centuries, Spain every four years, Poland and Russia every five.[99] But maybe we are going too far back in time. The two World Wars—only recently fought—caused 100,000,000 deaths, including 60,000,000 civilians. The Russian and Chinese Revolutions caused at least 50,000,000 more deaths; actually, historians have recently revised this figure upward to 100,000,000. As for the 146 little wars that have broken out since 1945, they have discreetly exterminated close to 30,000,000 people, three-quarters of them civilians, and most of those in the name of the world powers. The most distant of these places had histories no different from ours: over the course of its first six *centuries* of existence, China knew only seventeen years without war. In the course of its last century, China has endured Western colonialism, invasion by the Japanese, liberation, and successive Maoist revolutions: all told, China suffered an estimated 30,000,000 to 60,000,000 deaths. An astonishing article in the *Wall Street Journal* that called Deng Xiaoping the "Butcher of Tienanmen Square" knew little history. Those thousand innocent deaths in 1989 were fewer than the *daily* average death toll that China experienced over the sixty years of their late leader's public life. The article argued not for absolution but for a difference in viewpoints.

Only amazing arrogance can allow us to believe that the promulgation of Western values and their legal codification will prevent the return of war. As to the arguments that parties know their own best interests and act accordingly, they are all pathetic. Does anyone still believe, like Benjamin Constant in 1813, that "the more business dominates, the more war grows weak"? In 1912, Norman Angell demonstrated just as convincingly that a war with Germany was impossible.[58] It would seem that this rational pacifism of businessmen is ineradicable and infects even the wisest minds. Jean-Marie Guéhenno thus writes, in an otherwise remarkable lucid essay, that "more than ever prosperity will require order."[77] Of course. But why would order be peaceful? And what order are we talking about, anyway?

More Wars of Necessity than Wars of Ambition

Most of the world crises of the future will be political orphans. There will be no State with a political vision or Superpowers concerned to maintain global equilibrium to watch over them. Like the wars of ghetto children they will have no internal or external controls unless they threaten to overflow their boundaries. Contrary to what has been written so often, the Gulf War was not an example of what is to come, but rather the last chapter of what was. The war in Yugoslavia is the real harbinger, because it is a war without a State, a battle for survival where each side's very existence is seen as incompatible with that of the others. For a long time, this war only mattered because it was in danger of overflowing into Kosovo, and from there into Albania, maybe even into Greece. Preventing this risk from becoming reality is the only direct commitment—discreet but very serious—that the United States has yet made in Yugoslavia.

There are many such wars around the world. Some are well known; they embody ancient antagonisms that have finally been liberated by the crumbling of empires and by religious or nationalistic fanaticism. The former Soviet Union abounds in such conflicts: Ossetia and Georgia, Armenia and Azerbaijan, Uzbekistan and Tadjikistan, the last made worse by the adjacent Afghan conflict. The recent outbreak of conflicts in Africa offers a similar example: Angola, Rwanda, and Liberia are all suffering far more deaths than Bosnia, not to mention Niger, Sudan, and Somalia. But these countries, though obscure, are known. In others, as yet unknown to us, forces are silently at work that will lead their populations into unforgivable atrocities. These wars will find their own "good" reasons for happening, but they are really rooted in the simple inability of the parties to live together. Often, history or geography will give these conflicts an ethnic or religious aspect that will be presented as a cause for the war, even if it is only incidental to it.

The little-known conflicts in Mauritania and Senegal, for example, are the result not of ethnic conflicts but of a struggle for survival. There are already too many inhabitants per square mile and the population will double in less than two generations. The stakes are food and drink, and thus access to water. Most of the water in this area comes from the Senegal River, whose flood plain constitutes the only "bread basket" in the country. From this point of view, the current flood control project is an excellent idea. But the Mauritanians who are ethnic Arabs control all the access to the river's banks, which leaves the black Mauritanians, who are the majority in the region, without any recourse. The Arab population believe that, given their numbers and their level of settlement and land use, they could benefit from regular development aid—provided that they retain exclusive access to the river. The Arab Mauritanians have ensured their domination by stripping the black Mauritanians in the region of their nationality and then expelling them into Senegal. This has resulted in an increased repression of the Arab Mauritanians living in Senegal, including the closing of the 1,700 businesses that they controlled and stepped-up military operations against them. The Arab Mauritanians, in addition to their expulsion policy, have begun to intensify their ethnic cleansing.

A similar situation, just as little known but even more serious, prevails in Bangladesh, where the population is projected to grow from 120,000,000 to 240,000,000 in less than two generations. Today, the population density stands at 800 people per square kilometer (as if there were 450 million people living in France) on soil that is irrigated by floods and therefore very difficult to conserve. There is only 0.08 hectare [about 0.2 acre] of arable land per inhabitant, an area that will decrease to 0.03 hectare [about 0.075 acre] in less than forty years due to population increase and erosion. To put these figures into context, the equivalent ratio in Western Europe is 0.3 hectares [about 0.75 acre] per inhabitant, with a productivity six times higher. In other words, whereas each European has 3,000 square meters [about 32,300 square feet] to grow his food, each Bengali has only 130 square meters [about 1,395 square feet] today and will have only 50 square meters [about 538 square feet] in two generations. Today's area guarantees his survival only one year out of two on average, with water shortages or floods—both frequent—destroying a considerable portion of the harvest. The situation will therefore become physically unmanageable, and is already so in many places.

The result of this has been massive immigration from Bangladesh into Indian Assam. Fifteen million Bengalis have moved there; sometimes over half the population of a village. The Indians see them as plunderers. In 1983, a bad harvest year, a riot caused 1,700 deaths in five hours. The Indian government had to seize the property of thousands of Bengali families, some of whom had lived in Assam for two generations, in order to give their land to Indians, who have barely one hectare [about 2.5 acres] of arable land per inhabitant. These Bengalis were deported to Bangladesh, where they were not born but where their families took them in, thus creating tensions both at the borders and in some of the villages where the economy is very fragile indeed.

There is nothing exceptional about these two examples. In one generation, the area of arable land per inhabitant in East Asia will decrease from 0.15 to 0.10 hectares [that is, from about 0.4 acre to about 0.25 acre] and in Africa from 0.3 hectare to 0.1 hectare [or from about 0.75 acre to about 0.25 acre]. In China, it will diminish by half due to pollution and urbanization. Over this same period of time, water resources in some countries will also drastically decrease. The volume of water available per year will decrease by half in Iran, South Africa, Morocco, and Egypt, and by two-thirds in Nigeria, Ethiopia, Kenya and Libya.[27] In all these countries, the annual disposable quantity of water per capita will fall below 1,000 cubic meters [about 35,000 cubic feet] per inhabitant, that is to say ten times less than the contemporary French average: 600 cubic meters [about 21,000 cubic feet] in Egypt, 400 cubic meters [about 14,000 cubic feet] in Algeria, 300 cubic meters [about 10,600 cubic feet] in Tunisia, 200 cubic meters [about 7,060 cubic feet] in Kenya. By comparison, the Israelis of the West Bank, whose rural and urban water management is exemplary, consume about 1,500 cubic meters [about 53,000 cubic feet] per person per year; they estimate that it will be impossible for them to use less than 1,200 cubic meters [about 42,000 cubic feet] per person per year; this is the goal they have set for the year 2000 in their water conservation plan.

This problem is much worse in the cities. According to the World Bank, most developing countries have been able to give their peasants better access to water in the past twenty years.[27] Meanwhile, however, the situation in the cities has been getting progressively worse, due to their enormous growth. The urban population of the developing countries is increasing twice as quickly as their total population: by 6 percent per year in Africa or Southeast Asia, 4 percent per year in Latin America or South Asia. Ninety percent of the world's population growth in the next two generations will be in the cities. The cost of access to new water sources has doubled in fifteen years in Lima, Mexico City, and Algiers; it has tripled in cities in Central India, Jordan, and South China. In Shanghai between 1975 and 1990 the sources of water receded from the city center by 40 kilometers [about 25 miles]! The resulting tensions are developing into open conflicts: some between urbanites and rural dwellers, as on the West Bank of the Jordan, where the former divert water from the latter; others between the rich and the poor, as in Mexico City, where 60 percent of water consumption consists of illegal siphoning off in poor neighborhoods; neighbor–neighbor conflicts in countries with water sources as borders, where each side needs to control their common river exclusively in order to survive.

The Risk of War Is Not Just for the Poor

While the combination of such stakes as those and the breakdown of the State is bound to lead to wars, other factors contribute as well. The prosperity of industrialized nations is accompanied by a growing interdependence among them, which also brings many risks, less obvious but just as great. Just as the ideology of human rights is supposed to prevent ethnic or religious massacres, so the ideology of free trade is supposed to unify the whole planet in one vast wave of prosperity. The integration of the world economy is not a subject for debate. For everyone involved, prosperity is linked to open economies; national markets alone, even when they are as large as those of Japan and the United States, no longer suffice to assure the steady growth of national economies. This is all the more true for the more recently industrialized countries.

Many countries from Spain to Korea, including Tunisia and Mexico, have been able to industrialize thanks to a growth in their foreign trade that is much faster than that of their domestic economies. Serious commercial conflicts have resulted from this; the negotiations of the Uruguay Round made plain both their intensity and their bitterness. This inescapable integration will continue to give rise to serious differences, even political crises, among the industrialized countries and with their developing competitors, but it will probably not lead to any actual armed conflicts.

This integrated, interdependent, industrialized prosperity machine, however, also has a much more fragile flip side—its dependence on raw materials and supplies. The industrialized countries are transformers of raw materials, which are largely imported. It's not just a question of energy or raw materials, or of intermediate goods such as steel, plastics, or textiles, but also of spare and component parts. Large enterprises farm out their manufacturing stages in order to obtain the lowest possible production costs. Fully half of all of the world's industrial trade results from the transfer of spare and component parts between the different manufacturing plants of multinational businesses. No developed nation can remain competitive along the whole chain of production, especially when competing with the newly industrializing nations. The debates about social and ecological dumping are not going to end soon. Dependence on raw materials and supplies is a real national-security concern. Both Europe and Japan would suffer tremendously from the closing of the American market and vice versa. But they would all collapse completely if they lost access to their supplies of raw materials. Japan is the most extreme example of this vulnerability.[72]

Commercial conflicts are discussed in dollars, but security concerns are physical. That Japan's trade surplus in 1994 represents about $100 billion and one-third of her exports is a major political problem. That its imports take up 120 percent of the world's shipping capacity is a vital security issue for Japan, and felt as such. Look at Japanese elementary-school history books, where the attack on Pearl Harbor is still justified as a defense of Japan's threatened oil supplies. This dependence has continued to increase frenetically since the end of World War II. The tonnage of Japanese imports has *doubled* every ten years for the past forty years. Japanese imports represented 12 percent of world shipping capacity in 1953 and are ten times more than that today. This means that the rotations of freighters—which don't travel only for Japan—have to be as numerous as possible and their runs as short as possible. Japan's suppliers therefore need to be nearby, which limits their number: Japan has only two suppliers for chromium and bauxite; three for zinc and iron; four for lead, titanium, and coal; and five for its oil.

Japan, therefore, cannot choose its suppliers. The loss of any one of its main sources would have grave consequences for it. But the reverse is not true. Australia, for example, is Japan's number one supplier of raw materials, supplying two-thirds of its bauxite, half of its coal and its zinc, a third of its iron and manganese, and a quarter of its nickel. But none of these purchases represents more than 1 percent of the value of Australia's exports of those goods.* Thus, Japan is much more dependent on Australia for raw-material imports than Australia is on Japan for raw-material exports. This imbalance is even more marked in the case of Canada and China. These countries could conceivably stop selling to Japan from one day to the next, and only few of their businesses would suffer. By contrast, this would be a catastrophe for Japan. It would result in the distancing of Japan's raw-materials suppliers and make Japan even more dependent on the free passage of ships through a few key straits.

This is because Japan cannot choose its shipping routes any

---

*Except for coal, which represents 6.5 percent of all Australia's coal exports, and iron, at 3 percent of Australia's iron exports.

more than it can choose its suppliers. Half its supplies go across the Pacific Ocean, which is safe because it is wide open and is controlled by the United States. The same is not true of the Indian Ocean, which the other half of Japan's imports must cross. The Indian Ocean is closed and offers only one short route to Japan: via the Strait of Malacca. To travel via the straits south of Indonesia and north of Australia lengthens the route by over 2,000 kilometers [1,200 miles]. The only other alternative is to go around the south coast of Australia, and that would add over 8,000 kilometers [5,000 miles] to the trip. Japan's access to raw supplies would effectively be cut off due to the resulting delays. Therefore, the Strait of Malacca is Japan's jugular artery. Half the heavy-duty freighters and two-thirds of the oil tankers that pass through the Strait of Malacca are headed for Japan. Overall, one third of all of Japan's trade passes through it! As Korea, Taiwan, and China continue to develop, they will encounter risks of the same nature and even the same extent.

A cutoff of supplies is a serious threat that actually *increases* with a country's prosperity. It has been rarely used, but it always effective. The 1973 oil crisis is a good example, but it is not the only one. In 1979 the USSR threatened to off its titanium exports, which at the time represented 60 percent of the world's consumption. Titanium is indispensable to the aviation and aerospace industries: when this happened their stocks quickly but briefly plummeted. In 1986, Iran threatened to dynamite the Strait of Hormuz, as Iraq also threatened to do in 1991. In both cases the United States announced immediate military reprisals. In 1988, Indonesia closed for 48 hours all the main straits under its control, raising acute fears. In 1994 Indonesia obtained the official status of an archipelago, which legally places all the key straits within Indonesian territorial waters. Indonesia hastened to affirm its commitment to the free passage of shipping, thus hinting that this was something not to be taken for granted. . . .

Yet we still look at such fears somewhat condescendingly. The preceding examples mostly involve conspicuously aggressive or marginal countries. Otherwise, why would such things happen? We have a hard time getting over the rational notion that wars must happen for good reasons—that is to say, for reasons that *we* understand.

How could prosperous nations risk their development over what looks to us like a spur-of-the-moment impulse? In the end, we always come back to the reasonable idea that the economic and legal integration of countries guarantees their stability. Yet Montesquieu already wrote, "It is not the mind that forms opinions, but the heart." East Asia is the best example of this.

Prosperous, Integrated and Becoming Democratic—Asia at Risk of War

Southeast Asia is considered proof that economic integration combined with a network of legal agreements can result in stability and security. In fact, though, this region's stability owes nothing to the virtues of free trade and international law, and everything to the political-military integration that the United States has brought about.

Power broker and policeman when necessary, the United States has enabled the rancors and antagonisms of the East Asian mosaic to coexist without conflict. But that area presents a Yugoslavia-like problem—raised to the hundredth power. Two or three generations of a Titoist regime might have enabled Yugoslavia to become a nation. Several more decades of economic development may enable Asia to definitively exorcise its past. Economic interdependence, increasing political cooperation, and the democratization of countries slowly coming under the control of their middle classes may allow the region to stabilize. Will Asia be given this much time? Nothing could be less certain. What is certain, however, is that if left to itself, the region will drift into conflicts which the importance of the stakes and the virulence of the resentments and suspicions involved could quickly turn into war. The latent tension between Japan and its neighbors is a good example of a war waiting to happen.

We saw earlier that Japan's economic role has not earned that country any gratitude—but neither have its prudence or its political neutrality. And the American guarantees don't make any difference. It was the United States that guaranteed and brought about Japan's comeback by, from 1951 on, making its development aid to the countries of the region conditional on their purchase of Japanese goods. These goods were delivered by American ships, in order to avoid serious "incidents" at the mere sight of a Japanese flag. Japan is tolerated only in return for a political nonexistence that it must continually demonstrate. But the proof is never accepted.

Under pressure from the United States, Japan's military budget reached 1 percent of its GNP* for the first time in 1976, creating a general uproar. It is true that given the size of Japan's GNP, this 1 percent results in a military budget comparable to France's. A large portion of that, however, goes to finance the American military presence and comfortable conditions for its own military. This is the only way to recruit people into a profession that is both looked down upon and inbred: two-thirds of all Japanese officers are the sons of officers. Japan's rearmament in the past decade has been continually criticized and restricted by the Diet. When in 1988 Japan extended its air-sea patrol zone from 500 to 1,500 miles, at the express and public demand of the United States, the entire region went into shock. The idea of a Japanese military plane flying as far as the Philippines aroused general indignation. The prime minister of Singapore, a pillar of American foreign policy for over thirty years, denounced Japan's aggressive rearma-

---

*Or one-fourth that of the main NATO countries.

ment, its return to expansionism, and the need for preventive military measures. China and the Philippines became violently agitated at the thought of their activities being thus monitored. When Japanese minesweepers were sent into the Gulf in 1991 at the insistence of the United States, Indonesia protested the remilitarization of the Japanese shipping lanes and announced increased surveillance of its straits, which are vital to the Japanese. When, in 1993, a law was voted authorizing Japanese soldiers to participate in UN missions, Singapore, Malaysia, and China made venomous public declarations about the shortsightedness and irresponsibility of those who had encouraged this. "It's like giving liqueur chocolates to a reformed alcoholic," declared the prime minister of Singapore.

Conversely, Japan felt equally threatened by the development of the Indian Navy. Japan was extremely concerned when in 1988 India announced that it wanted to acquire a high-seas fleet and then in 1989 when it rented a nuclear submarine from the USSR. When high-ranking Japanese political and military officials were asked for comment, they all affirmed that this development could have no other purpose than to put pressure on, even to block, Japan's vital shipping lanes. Japan publicly expressed its fears in terms that were reassuring to no one. When they emphasized "the threat to regional stability represented by any action that might impede the free passage of shipping," the authorities in Tokyo were expressing themselves with unusual clarity.

Those authorities also clearly confirmed that Japan thinks of its foreign relations in terms of potential threats and wars. Under these conditions, it is of some concern to the countries of the region that Japan possesses absolute naval dominance there. Japan's fleet is unrivaled in Asia, except by that of the United States. Japan has made it clear that its naval power is the result of American demands, which is true. But it also adds that this is not particularly surprising for an island power that depends on shipping for its supplies. Again, this is not particularly reassuring in a region where many other countries are in a similar situation.

Japan is particularly vulnerable, given its prosperity and its desire for political appreciation in the region. But Japan is not alone. The People's Republic of China has also increasingly become a source of worry to its neighbors. They believe China to be capable of the worst actions, but certainly not the best. The countries that border China feel that she merits their suspicion, but not their respect or their support. In the past, China disturbed other countries with her policy of systematic destabilization, which extended from India to Vietnam. China was only officially recognized by Indonesia in 1990 and by Korea in 1992. Today, her neighbors fear the instability that may follow the death of Deng Xiaoping. China's declared intention to develop the most powerful navy in the region is not exactly conducive to relaxing the regional atmosphere, already clouded by the declarations of Japan. Beijing acknowledges that its military spending has tripled since 1988, but points out that it is still low, at $5 billion in 1993. But experts all believe that this figure is grossly underreported; they place the real figure at $20 billion.[32] For the first time since 1945 Australia, in its December 1994 *White Paper on Defense,* considered China to be its principal security risk, which justified an increase in the Australian armed forces. Immediately, in a complete turnaround, Australia declared Indonesia to be its partner, although until then it had been considered a potential adversary.

The increased presence of the Chinese Navy in the China Sea is a source of worry to the entire region that becomes more acute each year. In 1974 Beijing seized the Paracel Islets, in the northern part of the China Sea, from Vietnam. Starting in 1980, China began to recall her former claim to inalienable rights over the entire China Sea. In 1988 she took over six of the Spratly Islands, a string of little islands far from the Chinese mainland, between the Philippines, Vietnam, and Indonesia. And China did the same thing in 1995 at the northern boundary of Indonesia's territorial waters, very close to the huge Nahuna natural-gas deposit. All that with complete disregard for the treaty on the Law of the Sea—which Beijing has never ratified—and with no explanation, much to the consternation of its neighbors. An Indonesian diplomat complained that "We have received no answer or justification, only the affirmation that the Chinese presence in these waters is a historical reality."

And Beijing continues to release "historical studies" which conclude that China has lost more than 3,000,000 square kilometers [about 1,170,000 square miles] to its neighbors, who all feel a vague threat in such declarations. They know how quickly the Chinese can become aggressive—including, as in the 1960s, for domestic political reasons. The large size of the overseas Chinese community worries China's neighbors so much that at the last Pacific countries summit in November 1994, China had to reaffirm that it would never use that population to destabilize its neighbors. None of these countries sees a positive role for China. "The best thing China can do is to keep doing what it has always done: stay united and stay home," declared a former Thai premier, who is nevertheless pro-China.

Even though Asia's development and integration may be moving along rapidly, they have not yet been able to unify countries with such strong antagonisms politically. The unification of Asia through its prosperity is a dangerous illusion created by the strength and the duration of the American presence in the region.

Nothing guarantees that the United States will play an important role in the Far East forever. In fact that role is likely to diminish, for several reasons. The first reason is its economic withdrawal. On the one hand, Japan has overtaken the United States in every country in the region except the Philippines. Japan dominates the area economically, whether in investments, commerce, or development aid. On the other hand, the East Asian countries are increasingly turning toward one another instead of to the United States. The share of their exports that the countries of Asia now send to one another has gone from 28 percent to 40 percent since 1980, while the share they send to the United States has stagnated at 30 percent. For the most prosperous countries, the gap is even larger and even more in favor of intra-Asian trade. The Four Dragons export half again as much of their goods to Asia as to the United States (45 percent versus 25 percent). For the ASEAN countries, the gap is even larger—three times more (54 percent versus 18 percent)—and for China larger still at five times more (65 percent versus 12 percent).[95]

Given those conditions, the second reason for the American decline is political. Outside of military-political circles, many American leaders are wondering whether the situation has not reached the point where the United States today is simply serving as a policeman—at its own expense—for Asian businessmen. Asia's reluctance to finance its own defense only fans these doubts.

The third reason is military. The Pentagon defends the American presence in the area only tepidly. It refused to renew its lease on its two largest bases in the region, Subic Bay and Clark Field in the Philippines, claiming that the rent being asked was exorbitant. It is significant that Corazon Aquino did not believe the Americans could or would refuse to pay; their presence in the region is simply taken for granted by the postwar generation of young leaders. It is also significant that Filipino public opinion was mainly opposed to the renewal of those leases.

These forces are taking a direction similar to what is taking place in Europe. Here America is disengaging carefully, but the process is nonetheless accelerating. Both sides are readying themselves for the transition. The Americans are reducing their military bases and counting on very secure friends in the region (Singapore, Diego Garcia), on their ability to project an image of military might, and on receiving warning of a serious crisis well in advance. The Asians are preparing for the transition too. For three years the regional economic institutions—including the trans-Pacific ones—have seen their political and diplomatic importance grow. After long opposition, the United States now encourages this development, just as it now encourages the Europeans to take increased responsibility for their own security. Since 1993, the meetings of the Asia-Pacific Economic Co-operation Group (APEC) and of the Asian Forum have become true political meetings that gather together all of the region's heads of state. Their true goal is to organize the region's stability in order to compensate for the lessening commitment of the United States. The problem, therefore, lies not in the movement itself but in its consequences. These days, two of these consequences seem particularly troubling.

The first is that no political convergence really ties these countries together. Will their current goodwill toward one another survive a serious regional conflict? What will be the result of the Islamic game being played by several States such as Malaysia, Indonesia, and Brunei, which have no other motive but a dangerous attempt to regain political legitimacy? What overarching common interests can possibly unite Indonesia and Singapore, or Malaysia and the Philippines, when they are confronted with a religious conflict, the latter possibly provoked by the radicalization of Islam, which, although a minor concern until recently, is a real risk? Or with an ethnic conflict, which would provide the perfect excuse for China to intervene in a major way in the region? Beijing is adept at dealing separately with all its neighbors, playing on their mutual distrust, their common hostility towards Japan, and the desire of each to have a privileged relationship with China. The United States would certainly be reluctant to commit itself in such crises, which could drag on for years.

The second result of this movement is that it leaves Japan really isolated and torn between the demands of America and Asia. For Japan to wish to join in the integration of Asia would be quite natural at this point, but Japan is disliked and distrusted everywhere in Asia, from Korea to Burma. Also, China is not about to let Japan convert its economic prosperity into political power. Beijing is already doing a good job of creating suspicion about the motives behind the generous development aid that Japan has dispensed in the region. However, for Japan to stay on the periphery of an Asian continent that is otherwise integrating means that it must continue to depend solely on the United States. But the U.S., realizing this, is increasingly linking commercial and security issues, providing military protection in exchange for the opening of Japanese markets to U.S. goods. This attitude leaves the Japanese astounded at what they see as its shortsightedness. The overall result is that Japan sees itself as effectively isolated and walking a very narrow ridgeline trail. A state of mind in which, for everybody's sake, it ought not to be encouraged.

This overview of East Asia demonstrates that the peace advocated by businessmen and judges will not overcome the wariness of the nations. And the region in question happens to be the most dynamic and the most prosperous in the world. In Central or South Asia, in the Near East or the Middle East as in Africa, the logic of war is once again looking more and more natural against a similar background of weak States and nations that are largely unintegrated regionally and even within their own borders.

The weakness of States has serious consequences, whether for the harmonious integration of religions and ethnicities or for the management of scarce resources. War is certain to break out if, faced with "essential" national interests, no one speaks for or insists on the good of all. No legal mechanism will be able to prevent the types of crises we have just examined. To be convinced of this, we need only look at the general indifference surrounding the many crises in Africa and Central Asia today. Without States, which are the only possible intermediaries, the wars in those far-off places are incomprehensible, almost nonexistent for us. How many among us are aware, for example, that more people have been killed in Angola than in Bosnia? Who shows the slightest interest in the rioting in Assam or the water wars in Mauritania? And who would want to intervene in them? The present major crisis in Central Africa, on the border between Zaire and Rwanda, is a case in point. Thousands and thousands of people have died there; despite months of debate nothing has been done.

Beyond this return of ordinary wars, it is the change in their character that deserves examination. Indeed, there is no reason to believe that these conflicts fall into any of the same categories as the wars that we have thought so hard about over the past two centuries.

CHAPTER 9

The End of Limited Warfare

> It is always easier to make war than peace.
>
> —Georges Clémenceau, speech at Verdun, July 1919

An Obsolete View of War?

For the last several centuries, our conception of war has been political. Clausewitz explained this strikingly in his aphorism: "War is the pursuit of politics by other means." By their nature, such wars are *limited*. They are a choice of means in the service of a logic of force. World War I, which is farthest removed from this logic, is described as an aberration by Churchill.[65] Since 1945, the logic of certain death has pushed this conception as far as it will go. When we do away with conflict as an option, only diplomacy remains. The only goal of the Superpowers' nuclear strategy was to recreate the possibility of war through the idea of a limited nuclear war that would be sure to remain limited. This impossible certitude was the only guarantee of peace. This example also shows that the concept of limits concerns the goals of war and not its means or its consequences. It is not the use of fewer or less powerful weapons that defines a war as limited.

In spite of its primitive weapons, the Thirty Years' War decimated a third of the population of Europe; the probability of coming back unharmed from one of its campaigns was less than 10 percent, or three times less than from the Battle of Verdun. Most of

World War I was waged upon a limited territory, but it would be hard to call that war "limited."

Today the very idea of limited war is disappearing. Limited war assumes the previous existence of defined objectives: its very name creates a relationship between the means used and the ends desired. It is a political concept founded on an idea of equilibrium. From Metternich to Kissinger, war has never been a way of reshaping the picture of the world, but rather a means of touching it up or altering it slightly. Normal war is a means of negotiation, the most intense form of argument. It tries to weaken an opponent's will, not to annihilate him, and thus is completely different from total war—not a bargain-basement version of it. Limited war assumes a balance between the objectives and the means used to achieve them, therefore clear boundaries around the field of battle. By contrast, all wars waged on the basis of purely military considerations inescapably become total, in that their ultimate goal is the opponent's complete defeat. This distinction is slowly vanishing; the reason once again is the weakness of the States.

Waging a limited war assumes three conditions. The first is the identification of its political goals; the war effort should be adapted to these. The second is that these goals cannot be felt by one of the parties to put its vital interests in jeopardy. The third is that the political powers have effective control over the soldiers—including after the fighting has started. When we look at these conditions in the light of history, we find that they are very demanding and quite unlike the reality of today's world.

Limited War Assumes a Legitimate State

The first condition assumes a State that controls its political environment well, both at home and abroad. In its foreign relations, the State must make it clear that it does not wish to change the established order, simply to defend its legitimate interests. Today when all conflicts take place under the eyes of both the legal system and the media, this is of primary political importance; this disclaimer is necessary to gain a certain level of support from international officialdom, notably the permanent members of the United Nations Security Council. Israel has long been particularly successful in this area. The erosion of Israel's credibility since its invasion of Lebanon and the ensuing massacres has made it more sensitive to pressure and reduced its room for political maneuvering. The open clashes between the Israeli government and George Bush's— the latter supported by U.S. public opinion—brought to an end to the long period of political impunity that Israel had managed to secure for itself.

The international legal system cannot stop war, but nevertheless it must to convince the world powers of its legitimacy. To appear to be the aggressor is a source of isolation and of political defeat. There is almost no aggressive act that can be undertaken with complete impunity. When Iraq invaded Kuwait in August 1990, the United States quickly realized that it had to situate its response within the framework of the United Nations and appear to be formally mandated by it. Another example of the need for legitimacy, even by the strongest, may be found in Russia's efforts since 1992 to justify her military actions on the soil of her next-door neighbors. Russia has tried everything in her power to obtain for her operations the endorsement of international organizations. She has asked for OSCE observers in Azerbaijan and for UN observers in Georgia. She has used every opportunity possible to emphasize the good will behind her demands on the Baltic States in connection with her wish to defend Russian minority rights there. Without receiving such legitimacy abroad, which passes for an acceptable justification of their aims, aggressor countries are marginalized or even banned. Saddam Hussein's Iraq and Slobodan Milosevic's Serbia are excellent examples of this.

Legitimacy is also essential in domestic matters. It is easy to mobilize opinion when what is at stake is presented as a vital interest, much less so when the stakes are deliberately limited, and most difficult of all to avoid swinging from one extreme to the other. Everything pushes us in this direction: the logic of confrontation, the denouncing of an injustice that needs to be rectified, the evoking of the inequities of the adversaries . . . Justifying and carrying out a limited war assumes that the link between the State and the nation is strong. This link is obvious in democracies, but it is needed in all countries, especially when they have to be mobilized.

A weak State will therefore have a hard time waging a limited war. Such a war will immediately be denounced as a domestic political stratagem. The weak State may hope that, on the contrary, the urgency of a total war will be stronger than a population's animosity towards its power; this will lend it some legitimacy, not only at home but also in the eyes of other countries. Thus in 1987 Rajiv Gandhi—prime minister of India and seriously weakened by a major corruption scandal—was told by his close advisors that he could make his troubles go away by launching a total war on Pakistan. Such a move could be easily justified by pointing to Pakistan's imminent acquisition of nuclear weapons, which could be a great threat to India. Pakistan's hardened attitude towards India since 1994, particularly regarding Kashmir, follows the same logic. Incapable of pushing through difficult but necessary reforms and overwhelmed by the strength of the new Muslim movements which the powers that be had long encouraged, Benazir Bhutto, before her electoral defeat in February 1997, appeared to be more and more tempted by a foreign adventure. In such critical periods, showing that one has the support of the populace establishes the legitimacy of both one's own claim and that of the State. The success of the king of Morocco's "Green March," which drew hundreds of thousands of Moroccans to demonstrate in favor of a Moroccan Sahara, is a striking example of this. What seemed at first to be nothing more than the personal whim of an absolute monarch soon became the demand of an entire people. This march was very instrumental in turning the diplomatic tide in Morocco's favor. Slobodan Milosevic's easy victory during the 1992 elections in Serbia solidified his status in international relations as well as that of his cause. Serbia's ambition and desire to rule did not become more acceptable, but her determination became more credible.

Limited War Assumes Goals that Everyone Involved Perceives as Limited

A convincing formulation of the political goals that the State is pursuing is therefore indispensable and presupposes a solid State power. Such a formulation is also the key to the second condition of a limited war, which distinguishes it unmistakably from an all-out war. The more the ends and their means merge, the more inevitable it is that the war will get out of hand. If a country thinks that its aggressor's motives and ambitions threaten its vital interests, then there will be an all-out war—a war not for specific national interests but for survival. In this case, the aggressor has two choices: either commit itself, with grave risks, or back off and suffer the consequences of a miserable political defeat at home. It would be a mistake to assume that any limited war has to become an all-out war simply because of one party's impending defeat. That escalation happens only if the political goal—and thus that war's limits—has not been well defined or has changed because of approaching victory.[83] Uncertainty about the outcome leads to fighting "to the last man." By contrast, defeat may be acceptable if its price is known and if that price is clearly distinguishable from the consequences of continuing, and losing, an all-out war. Moderation on the part of the victor—that is, when the victor keeps to its original demands—gives the vanquished the opportunity to work out an honorable outcome.

The Sino-Vietnamese War of 1979 provides a good example. China finally won on the battlefield, but its regular army paid a very heavy price, even though they had to deal only with Viet-

namese militia forces. Because of its military ineffectiveness, if
China had had to continue, it would have had to wage all-out,
total war. The Vietnamese understood the risk that they faced perfectly well and negotiated an honorable way out, defeated but not
humiliated. France's war against Libya in Chad provides another
example. The French had clear objectives in this conflict; they
stated them openly; the conflict was put into a context of international law; all these things allowed the French to limit their commitment, while not holding back within those limits, and at the
same time allowed the Libyans to withdraw without feeling threatened. Even more obvious was the limited nature of the Falklands
War between Argentina and the United Kingdom. Conversely,
many wars in the past were all-out wars because it was not clear to
any of the combatants what they were fighting for. In Europe, the
Thirty Years' War and World War I are extreme examples of this.
Others, farther east, are the Iran-Iraq War of 1981–1987 and the
Afghan War of 1979–1989.

A Limited War Cannot Be Left to the Military

Those two conflicts illustrate well the difficulty of the third condition, which is the permanent authority of the political power over
the military. Limited war involves delicate coordination between
the political and the military. Both in the conception and the exercise of war, the political authorities must continually deal with the
military logic of maximum efficiency at the lowest cost. Any cut-
back is always seen by the military as dangerously impeding one or
another of their goals. The only way to overcome this problem is to
closely integrate the civilian and military authorities and to truly
subordinate the latter to the former.

Otherwise, the working out of the war plans will consist of leaving the execution entirely up to the military, counting on them to
do that much and no more. The chances that they will actually do

this *and no more* are very slim. Actually, the military's subordination to political power is even more essential as the war goes on.
The military must commit as much power as necessary—but no
more—and power must never become an end in itself. This requires the commanders to have a clear vision of their objectives and
the political leaders to have the means to define them.

Otherwise, the military leaders may just shake off the political
goals in the name of effectiveness, as they were so often tempted to
do during the Korean War. Or, conversely, they may become para-
lyzed to the point of being unable to take advantage of a clear military superiority, as the Vietnam War demonstrated for the United
States.

The powerlessness of the United Nations in Bosnia illustrates the
insurmountable difficulties that arise when military goals are not
subordinated to and integrated with political ones. This is an almost cartoonish example, since there the political and military efforts are being carried out by different institutions. On one side we
find the United Nations and its blue helmets, whose policy is to
avoid all confrontation. General Lapreslc, the commander of the
French contingent, has said, "I have no adversary, I have only partners." On the other side stands NATO and its military troops,
whose logic is all the more theoretical because NATO has no soldiers in the field.

The two organizations cannot coordinate their efforts because
they lack an overarching political authority. The United Nations is
supposed to have one but it is powerless to overrule the NATO military organization, which operates on its own closed circuits. The
civilian members of NATO—its secretary-general and its council of
ministers—have absolutely no control over the NATO military,
who report only to their commander, who is American. He takes his
orders from Washington and nowhere else. NATO is really only
good at doing what it was originally set up to do: waging all-out war

against the USSR. By its very nature, NATO is incapable of waging a limited war as complex as the one in Bosnia. NATO is all the more powerless because the United Nations has no clear policy. The United Nations would like to show fairness occasionally, but in a way that does not commit it to action, because it does not feel it has a mandate to wage war. As a result, it gets involved in endless debates on issues as serious as aerial bombardments.

A Western general in Bosnia clearly analyzed the insurmountable nature of these conflicts between the United Nations and NATO. Regarding the air raids, he noted that "The UN is not responsible for this lack of response. It's NATO that refuses to lead bombing raids because numerous antiaircraft batteries have been spotted. NATO then decides that it wants to lead only massive strikes in order to avoid the risk of losing several aircraft. But then it's the UN that refuses to authorize a massive strike because it wants to stay in the negotiation mode." That numerous French officers on the ground have said "Let's shoot or bug out" does not mean they are spoiling for a fight; it only shows the impossibility of fighting a limited war in such conditions. What is needed is a combination of delegation and subordination, of confidence and authority, which assumes a very strong political control over the military.

The weakening of the States, however, often shows itself in a heavy reliance on the military—who are often kept in the background for public-relations reasons. This is the tribute paid to democratic appearances, but it is hard to ignore the reality. From China to Peru, from Algeria to Russia there are very few weak States that do not depend on the military to keep them in power, in exchange for the right to do as they please. The examples of such military autonomy given in the preceding chapter are a strong indication of the reliance of weak States on their military forces—which are even afforded some immunity from the penal laws of certain weak States in return for their essential support.

The breakdown of States begins by benefiting the military and ends up encouraging wars.

The Utopian Legal System—the Source of Total War

The strong political structures needed to wage limited wars do not exist today, except in a handful of countries that are little inclined toward this type of war anyway. Elsewhere, the very nature of the way States function—more than the personal ambitions of tyrants—assures that wars will be total. This is above all the result of the multiplication of artificial States that were founded only because of the will of a group of people who wished to set themselves apart from neighbors with whom they were in conflict. They "don't know what they're building as a group any more, but they know whom they hate absolutely."[80] The disastrous results of the utopian legal system are now becoming quite apparent. The political map that it is drawing is no longer built on affinities but rather on clashes. It's not borders that are being drawn any more but battle lines. The transformation of minorities into States makes their confrontations go straight from political crises to all-out wars. Total war, actually, is similar to civil war: it represents the absolute refusal of a certain political order and the inner conviction that survival is at stake. It is no longer a question of touch-ups but rather of redrawing the portrait of the world.

We have a difficult time comprehending this phenomenon. Some write about the "disunity of nations," others of a return to the Middle Ages, still others of a "war of civilization."[47] All of these references are wrong. The breakdown of States changes the nature of war. Medieval wars—the so-called wars of civilization—were long-drawn-out butcheries, but they were based on firm political goals. From the eight centuries of war between Islam and Christianity to the European wars of succession in the seventeenth and eighteenth centuries, to the secular Sino-Mongolian and the no less secular

Sino-Chinese civil wars, political goals are found everywhere. Read *The Romance of the Three Kingdoms,** a brilliant novel that recounts four centuries of China's disintegration starting in the third century A.D., to see just how important political objectives were in those interminable combats.

Contemporary wars—those that threaten to break out everywhere—are more wars of survival than power struggles. They come about not from calculated bids for power, but instead from gut fear. The breakdown of the States is dividing society into entrenched camps. Each tries to find security with their own kind, following an inexorable logic of the tribe or the clan. Whether it's about race, religion, or territory, the same fear of the "other" is at work, a fear that only death can exorcise. Sudan, Rwanda, Liberia, or Angola in Africa; Azerbaijan, Tadjikistan or Afghanistan in Central Asia; Bosnia in Europe; or Sri Lanka in South Asia: all are ongoing examples of such inchoate total wars.

The era of political wars is coming to an end. In the future such wars will remain the privilege of the great powers, which will only rarely engage in them. The unwillingness of public opinion to tolerate casualties and repressed guilt about the use of power so influence the course of events that only when obvious and immediate interests are at stake will the reluctance to fight be overcome. The "duty" to intercede in other countries' affairs has no future. The Somalian adventure is probably the last of its kind for quite a while, especially for the great powers. No one is likely to do the same thing in Nigeria or in Sudan.

On the other hand, the exercise of real protective guardianship seems to be on the increase. Since 1986, the United States has intervened three times in its immediate sphere of influence: in Grenada,

---

*Kuan-Chung Lo, *The Romance of the Three Kingdoms,* translated by C. H. Brewitt-Taylor (C. E. Tuttle, Rutland, VT, 1988), a Chinese narrative of the sixteenth century [Translator's note]

Panama, and Haiti. Since 1990, Russia has led an impressive series of military actions in its vicinity. More than 30,000 Red Army soldiers are stationed in Georgia, Moldova, and Tadjikistan, without counting all the "technical assistants" and other advisors present there. France maintains about 15,000 soldiers in Africa. And so on. These interventions, however, are limited and case-by-case. The countries doing the intervening possess crushing military superiority and strong political control in the countries they have entered. In fact, these interventions are not wars as such, but rather police actions, made possible by a vital interest and a low perceived risk. The commitments of the superpowers will not exceed this level in the future.

Because of the breakdown of States, the unwillingness to make military commitments and the desire for order will lead to new solutions. If necessary, these solutions will violate legal principles that were supposedly sacrosanct. Thus, we are already seeing countries consent to camouflaged forfeiture of their sovereignty, as in Lebanon, Sri Lanka, or Tadjikistan. Tomorrow, we will probably see the abandonment of the concept of borders, the last inheritance of nineteenth-century geopolitics and the order of the Cold War. What do the borders of Bosnia or Moldova mean today? And tomorrow, those of Georgia or Ukraine? If South Africa remains the strongest economic and military power on the African continent, what will its neighbors' borders be worth?

Increasingly, the term *limited war* will come to mean *local war* and little else. History clearly teaches that such wars are in fact without limit. The Battle of Cannae in 216 B.C., fought entirely wiith swords and lances, claimed over a hundred thousand deaths in two days. The naval battle of Lepanto in 1571 caused the death of 16,000 people in one day; this remains a record for a sea battle. In the sixteenth and seventeenth centuries, it was not uncommon for 20 to 25 percent of the fighting forces of armies to be annihilated in one battle.[99] You have to be suffering from the comfortable amnesia brought on by fifty years of peace to forget humanity's endless tolerance for warfare.

And There's No Reason Why
Such Wars Won't Be Nuclear

And why would future wars not be nuclear? Certainly not for lack of capability. To possess the quantity and type of weapons that France or the United States has today is a huge and expensive technological undertaking. But it costs much less to make just one large bomb and keep it in working order. The basic models used on Hiroshima or Nagasaki can be ordered today by mail. This is not an exaggeration: accurate plans for these two models are in the public domain. They were made public because of the "wholesale" declassification of the American archives from the 1940s. There has been worse: some key instructions for constructing a thermonuclear weapon were recently published—accidentally—in a U.S. magazine. The American security services, at first horrified, started by banning their publication and recalling the already published plans; then they realized that publicity would only make the situation worse. The limited distribution of the magazine (which is only one among many), as well as its rather secondary importance, lead them to hope that this leak will soon be forgotten. Not much of a safeguard . . . As for first-generation nuclear weapons, workable plans are not only available but easy to improve upon, because of the many advances in both electronic and metallurgic technology since such weapons first appeared. This means that just about anybody can produce crude versions of these weapons, compact but deadly. Their power is known only approximately: 10,000 or 20,000 or 30,000 tons of TNT. What's the difference?

The real strategic change is that nuclear testing is no longer required to produce a primitive but operational nuclear weapon. This is a truly radical change that has not yet been fully understood. Until recently, everyone thought that chemical weapons would be the poor countries' nuclear weapons. But we have to come to terms with the fact that from now on, the poor countries' nuclear weapons will be . . . nuclear weapons. Still, they are not within everyone's reach—for several reasons.

First of all, knowhow is one thing, but actually producing nuclear weapons is another. The engineering of a basic nuclear bomb is not simple; it assumes a body of very advanced knowledge. Then you need fissionable materials of military quality. Buying them is not easy, although the increase in supplies resulting from the Russian-American disarmament makes their illegal sale much more common. Producing them is not easy either. But here too the basic techniques are well known and, with patience, yield good results. After all, whether in terms of quality or quantity, the emerging nuclear powers don't have the same ambitions for their weapons as the established nuclear powers have for theirs: diversification, miniaturization, and precision are unimportant to them. Finally, all this assumes huge amounts of money: to build the laboratories and factories, to buy or steal equipment, technologies, and materials costs billions of dollars. But is this ever a permanent barrier?

None of what has been just described is easy or quick. There will not be fifty—or even twenty—nuclear powers overnight. In 1961 the CIA predicted that situation for 1970, and in 1974 again predicted that situation for 1990. Stealing such weapons is unlikely and moreover useless, because the safety devices that prevent them from firing are to all intents and purposes impregnable. To produce these bombs is difficult and expensive. But it is possible: if there are ten nuclear powers in the future instead of five, the world picture changes dramatically. That day may not be far off. India and Pakistan are coming inexorably closer to it. Both are past the stage of just acquiring knowledge and have begun to build up an arsenal. In 1992, the Union of South Africa announced simultaneously that it possessed the ability to produce nuclear weapons and that it would not do so. Several months later, South Africa signed the Treaty on the Nonproliferation of Nuclear Weapons (NPT) as a nonnuclear State. Without giving any details as to its nuclear status, Brazil had expressed the same nonnuclear intentions the preceding year. An analysis of Iraq's inventory showed that it was only a year or two away from being able to produce first-generation nuclear weapons. As for the countries that have the technical and economic resources to become nuclear powers, they are easy to list.

That nuclear weapons exist is one thing. That they should be used is quite another. What rational thinking could possibly justify the use of nuclear weapons in tomorrow's wars that would make such a use more likely than it was yesterday?

In order to answer this question, we need first to change our viewpoint on "the bomb." For over fifty years, we have considered it an uttermost limit, the farthest reach of war. The logic of certain death imposed this viewpoint on us; it froze out the use of the bomb because its use meant the death of everyone. What would happen if we could limit the number of deaths? If nuclear war were to become limited, then it would no longer mean the end of history. If they can be used in a limited way, nuclear weapons return to being just that—weapons. They are not just any weapons, but then again all-out wars are not waged for just any stakes.

Indeed the stakes in total wars are eerily similar to the pillars of Gaullist deterrence: the imperatives of territory and freedom of action. One of this doctrine's founding fathers explained this, emphasizing its breadth: "In defending the autonomy of French strategy, we are defending more than just our territory: the possible shape of a strategy with a universal value."[100] He did not see that doctrine's depressing decline.

Thirty years later, his thoughts were echoed by the chief of staff of India, who was asked what lessons he'd learned from the Gulf War. "Never fight the United States without nuclear weapons," he answered. The original French doctrine is permeated with the sanctification of territory, in the double sense of its inviolability and its sacredness. "In strict political and strategic logic, a vital interest is synonymous only with protecting the nation's territory."[100] Lucien Poirier, a purist theoretician in matters of Gaullist doctrine, defines a vital interest as "the sacred, that which a people recognizes as necessary to its unity and to its uniqueness, the reason why it exists and says it ought to live."[101] Pronounced by General de Gaulle, these words comfort the nation and act as a warning to potential enemies. Declaimed by Saddam Hussein, they remain just as intense, but change their meaning. When the breakdown of States is combined with the absence of any international order, leaving only collective raw emotions, when nuclear death ceases to be universal but the means of causing it become so, it is difficult to imagine that the same logic that fueled nuclear deterrence yesterday will not fuel nuclear use tomorrow.

The French believed with all their hearts in the power of nuclear arms to inspire reasonableness. As late as 1994, the French *White Paper on National Defense* mentions "the horror that they inspire" as reducing the risk of these weapons being used.[5] There may well be a logic behind nuclear weapons, but why just one? Already in 1952, George Kennan, then American ambassador to Moscow, warned his government: "Nothing guarantees that the reasoning of our opponents is the same as our own. How could we assume such a thing about the leaders of a country whom we suspect are ready to place the bet of a nuclear attack, when they cannot calculate the odds of such a bet?"[85] The Cold War answered this question. It showed that the USSR subscribed to the same world order as the United States, even if it wanted to change its hierarchy. From this time on, Henry Kissinger estimated that the real risk of a nuclear world was posed by those States that did not want this order tidied up but instead overthrown in favor of another order more to their liking. Those are the real stakes from now on.

Only Strong States Can Prevent the Use of Nuclear Weapons

Revolution is not necessarily subversion. At the beginning of the 1960s the Superpowers feared that China would launch a world-wide campaign of subversion. This fear was given credibility by the rhetoric of the Chinese leadership, which boasted of China's invulnerability due to its size and the wide dispersion of its population. The warlike tone of these declarations and the anarchy of the country added weight to these concerns. Revolution from now on is about overturning political and military concepts. The end of the concept of limited war means a change in nuclear thinking. The true risk is not what we used to imagine, that is, an act of aggression against the principal powers by some atomic desperado. This type of scenario lets one create a "threat from the South" and an artificial solidarity in the developed North.

The real danger is more subtle: already the nuclear thinking of the new powers is more military than it is political. In 1975, James Schlesinger, then U.S. Secretary of Defense, concluded that "the choice of proliferation is a choice of a doctrine of use."[21] In 1987 François Mitterrand came to the same conclusion, emphasizing that "[I]f any nuclear weapon escaped the logic of deterrence, that would mean that people's thinking had been so distorted that they were already obsessed with its use, how it should be used, as if the war had already started."[18] Everything today supports these analyses: the evolution of the political environment and of the logics of war, as well as technical reasons that make these factors more dangerous.

The political management of nuclear arms and the dangerous game of deterrence assume that a strong political power will be backed up by a flawless technical system. This civilian control center must be informed of everything very early on, and without mistakes: about the risk, then the reality and the form of the attack. Without this intelligence, governments are powerless to act, because they must either strike preemptively or wait to be hit at the risk of losing all their capacity to strike back. Guaranteeing this quality of intelligence is extremely difficult. Only the United States and the USSR have invested enough money to give their leaders this much lead time. And anyway the problem under consideration was a relatively simple one. The attack was expected to be massive and to come from far away, and the weapons were assumed to be easily recognizable high-trajectory missiles. To detect without error small, commonly seen vehicles such as airplanes, which would give little warning because they would be coming from a neighboring country, is much more complicated. An important part of the American "Star Wars" program was devoted to this very problem. Solutions were found—as evidenced in the Gulf War—but they proved to be extremely complicated.

The situation is even more serious for emerging powers because of their fragility. In order to guarantee the thorough destruction of their enemies, the two Superpowers had built up an enormous arsenal. But according to the director of Pakistan's nuclear program, a mere dozen bombs aimed at key targets in India or in Pakistan would suffice to send those two countries back to subsistence level. Maybe the real figure is twenty or thirty key targets, but in any case it is a very low number: this explains the special nervousness of these governments. Moreover, surveillance activity itself can contribute to the tension. During the Cuban missile crisis, the U.S. Navy, acting on its standing crisis orders, had located and targeted all the Soviet nuclear submarines, which were few at the time. This surveillance could have appeared highly threatening and have provoked a Soviet response, which, in turn, could have led to an action by the U.S. Navy, which would then have been left with no alternative to direct confrontation.

Those in power, however, must be sure that they have the power to act, otherwise their authority will be meaningless. Even today, the most modernized armies have areas of astonishing ineffectiveness. Most of the consequences are never made public, but they provide food for thought—such as the "accident" that happened to the American electronic-surveillance ship *Liberty,* sunk by the Israeli Air Force in 1967. Israel had warned the U.S. government that the *Liberty* had gotten too close to a security zone. After discussion, the Pentagon agreed to ask its ship to withdraw, because the Israelis had threatened to attack it. The Pentagon sent the *Liberty* four messages in thirteen hours; none reached the ship. The first was mistakenly sent to the Philippines. The second—strangely enough—was routed through the American intelligence eavesdropping services, which simply thought it was an erroneous message and filed it. The third was lost by a defective relay at U.S. Navy headquarters in the Mediterranean; and the fourth was delayed because it had been mistakenly coded "non-urgent," but it eventually arrived. Meanwhile the Israelis, convinced of the bad faith of the United States, sent the ship to the bottom with all hands.

In 1975, an American troop-transport ship was intercepted by Cambodian guerrillas on May 12. The ship had been trying to inform American forces on land of its predicament, but their radio frequencies were not compatible. A U.S. Air Force plane discovered this situation by chance but could not contact the ship, for the same reason. The next day the information about the ship finally reached Washington, which decided to launch a rescue mission, provided that the ship remained in the same location. Unfortunately, the military telecommunications satellite that was supposed to transmit these instructions was defective. It took time for Washington to realize this and to reroute the message via the NATO satellite, which sent it to Thailand. For obscure reasons, the message was finally sent to the American ground troops on the night of the 13th via the public telephone system. The Cambodians were thus able to learn all the details of the operation. They prepared a warm reception: 41 marines were killed and 50 were wounded. Meanwhile, the Cambodians had loaded the American equipment onto an airplane that had been on its way to the United States when the attack took place, thus adding political humiliation to the military fiasco.

The leaders of the nuclear powers have been obsessed—and rightly—with the problem of message transmission, an area where only perfection will do. Without perfect communications they must give up the power to make decisions or delegate it to the military. Among the emerging powers, no government possesses technical means sufficient for it to assure its military that it can make and transmit sound decisions in real time. Queried on this subject, the chief of staff of Pakistan comments, "Faced with this risk, we have no other choice than to launch on warning."

This technical limitation forms a part of the political context of weak States. Control of their nuclear programs is entirely in the hands of the military, who are anyway the mainstays of these regimes when they don't actually run them. In Iran the autonomous management of these programs has run uninterruptedly since 1976, in spite of a tempestuous political revolution. Zulfikar Ali Bhutto's ambition when he was prime minister of Pakistan to impose government control on his country's nuclear program was one of the major reasons for his overthrow by the military, who also threatened to overthrow his daughter, the recently ousted prime minister Benazir Bhutto, if she tried to meddle in nuclear matters in her turn. In Brazil a high-ranking official confided in an interview that the president's decision to end that country's nuclear program was the best way for him to gain control over it—he had had none before.

A Return to the Obvious: A Nuclear Weapon Is . . . a Weapon

This attitude is not just the result of the military's thirst for power.

For these men, weapons are weapons, not symbols. They have a very Gaullist notion of deterrence. Their awareness of how vulnerable they are, and that they have no margin for error, renders irrelevant the type of diplomatic fist-shaking which is the only use we have made of nuclear weapons. In such weak States, nuclear weapons play the same role as other weapons in assuring the nation's safety and its ability to achieve its essential goals. There is no longer anything unique about nuclear weapons, except an acute sense of vulnerability that is only sharpened by the will to use them.

We have become so unused to thinking of nuclear weapons as weapons that any reasoning to the contrary outrages us. Yet a glance at history reminds us that every nuclear power has had a first-strike policy. It may have been a well-kept secret, but it was very real. The United States, for example, never announced such a policy, but its existence was confirmed more than once and early on. In 1953, during the Korean War, President Eisenhower let it be known that he was prepared to envisage a first-strike attack against China; the message was passed along via Moscow. He repeated this message in 1958, this time via Delhi, during the crisis over Quemoy and Matsu. In 1975, the American secretary of defense stated to a Japanese newspaper that the United States was not discounting the possibility of a preventive strike in Korea.[29] Four years later, his successor admitted for the first time that U.S. nuclear doctrine included an official first-strike option.

In France, contrary to popular opinion, General de Gaulle never ruled out this possibility. Interviews with some of his key advisors reveal that he too saw a military role for these weapons, whose diversity he had guessed and whose flexibility of use he had imagined early on. His no-nonsense pragmatism made it impossible for him to rule out the possibility of a limited use for them. The Warsaw Pact's doctrine was also a doctrine of use. The use of nuclear weapons was completely integrated into the conduct of their war operations. Soviet military plans seized in the former East Germany have proved as much. The commitment of nuclear weapons was planned on an immediate basis, and the military had very broad authority as to their use—which confirms that they were considered combat weapons. The sheer size of Russia's task in collecting these tactical weapons to disarm them, starting in 1991, shows just deeply they permeated its entire military system.

Doctrines of nuclear use do not necessarily reflect a militarism gone mad. These doctrines are realistic in seeing nuclear weapons for what they really are: weapons. This does not prevent politics from playing a role, nor does it compel the use of nuclear weapons at the outset. But it does not forbid them either, and that changes everything. Fifty years of "minor" wars have already taught us that nuclear weapons do not prevent wars. We shall discover that they do not prevent nuclear wars either. They only prevent all-out nuclear wars between those who can make wars all-out.

CHAPTER 10

The Doctrinal Imperative

From now on a yawning gap exists between the quest for
complete peace and the military doctrine of all-out war.

—Henry Kissinger

A Forgotten Requirement

For half a century nuclear weapons have hypnotized us. Suddenly jolted awake, we now realize that all over the world people are cutting one another's throats in the streets. Everywhere we look, small wars are raging, quietly but brutally and with no end in sight. This sudden wake-up call has left us dazed and confused. Long immobilized by the absolute impossibility of war, we are now experiencing war on a daily basis. The common language of nuclear war that once kept it in check is no longer spoken. These new wars that are erupting and massing on the horizon have little to do with strategy or ideology and have everything to do with gut emotions. They are no longer a political option but an organic necessity. The blood they are spilling so profusely is intolerable to us; secretly we find it vulgar. We are still proclaiming: "The main goal of defense is the maintenance of identity and independence."[5] But then to turn around and disembowel one another over an acre of land, a hamlet, or some ancient totem . . . !

What we thought was the next stage in history was only a parenthesis. The inexorable coherence of the logic of mutual assured destruction led us to believe that force had finally given us a universal language: the nuclear weapon had put an end to Babel. Under these conditions there was no more need for a military doctrine, just as there would be no more need for religion if God became visible. When weapons have reached the point where everyone must follow the same reasoning, strategy becomes only a question of how. Only absolute force can create a single lingua franca of war. Nuclear weapons in and of themselves are not enough; in its perfect simplicity, only certain death for everyone was able to accomplish this. We have no other universal logic. By theorizing about war being "nuclear-and-therefore-impossible," we convinced ourselves that our reasoning mattered, when in fact the only thing that mattered was death.

The comeback of all-out wars has shown in five years what we had forgotten for over fifty: force alone does not create any shared concept of rationality. In their ways, Iraq and Bosnia have proved as much. In spite of unanimous condemnation, an international embargo, and an armada stationed on his doorstep, Saddam Hussein has made a calculated, rational political decision quite different from what this enormous mobilization might normally have suggested to him. Today, Serbia is doing the same thing. And yet— Serbia is blithely risking the possibility of a response by NATO, the strongest military power in the world, the power that was able to push back the Soviet Union itself!

The fact that we thought even for a moment that military force was equivalent to politics shows how much the two things have become confused in our minds.

That is why nothing is more important than the formulation of a new, appropriate doctrine. For the role of doctrine, as Henry Kissinger said, is just that: to translate force into politics. For that is the purpose of a doctrine: it decides when the stakes are worth the use of force and how much force is justifiable to defend them. Doctrine is the permanent setting forth of ends and means. Only the extraordinary case of total nuclear war was able to do away with doctrines or reduce them to tautologies. In every other case, the existence of a doctrine is the prerequisite for any display of independent power.

The great nations' freedom to act is becoming dangerously limited as compared to their military might and this gap is growing rapidly. This "divorce" of military might and political power is serious: not knowing how to use the former properly condemns us to abandon the latter. We have only to look at the bitter skepticism that greeted the military-purchase-planning law of 1994 in France, which was passed just when Gorazde was being abandoned to the Serbian forces. The inability of the major powers to assume their responsibilities creates not appeasement but only a vacancy on the world scene. The crises to come will be more difficult to respond to than those of the Cold War: they will be crucial to the protagonists, but they will seem distant to us. In those all-out wars, no one will want to sign treaties—the wars in Bosnia and Central Asia show this clearly. And not wanting peace is an advantage in war: it allows you to wait out your opponent. This strategy was used by the Soviets in the past and the Serbs today; its effectiveness is obvious. Without a doctrine, that is, without a definition of both the stakes and the limits, we are condemned to make a series of concessions. Only a firm doctrine can back up a patience that needs to seem infinite to our adversaries. The Western successes against Iraq and Libya are due to the West's having both a clearly articulated, consistent policy and the appropriate means to carry it out. Without a doctrine, military might becomes doubly captive: to powerlessness and to emotion.

The International System: An Organization Without Order

A national doctrine of the use of force is not formulated in a vacuum. It depends on other countries' conceptions as well. It also depends on common principles that countries work out in the course of their relations with one another. These few rules define the nature of the order of international relations at any given time. In the past, these were just the overall result of the various balances of power. To adhere to them did not necessarily mean ratifying every single element of the status quo, but holding to the principles behind it and its global balance. Within the limits of this balance, the goal of the policies of the States was to negotiate arrangements that would be most favorable to themselves. The order was therefore *conventional* in nature. This conception of international relations emerged from the ruins of Napoleonism and came to an end in the ruins of the Berlin Wall. In between, it prevailed for more than two centuries in spite of a great many crises and changes.

This stability is due to the fact that the geopolitical arrangements changed remarkably little during this time. Between 1815 and 1989, there were very few States capable of being real players on the international scene, and their number has been decreasing. In the nineteenth century, the world map was radically simplified. By 1900, there were only two independent countries in Africa—Ethiopia and Morocco—and four in Asia—Siam (Thailand), Afghanistan, Japan, and China. And their independence was extremely fragile and was protected by policies of extreme prudence. The situation hardly changed until 1945.

Over the next fifty years, the growth in the number of States did not affect that concept, and international relations were dominated by the presence of nuclear arms and by the relationship between the two nuclear Superpowers. The exclusivity of this dyad of the Superpowers deprived the grand organizational plans of the postwar period of all their meaning. The world order had never been so simple or so conventional. This Metternich-like conception of international order came to an abrupt end in 1989. But the difficulty that we have encountered in coming up with another viable doctrine of the proper use of military force is not only due to the suddenness or the scope of the change. It is also the result of major misreadings of the nature and workings of the international order of today.

It seemed for a moment that the fall of the Berlin Wall would at last allow the international system as conceived in 1945 to function as it was meant to. The Cold War had jammed the system, but its underlying principles were still valid. The supremacy of international law, the intangibility of borders and sovereignties, the integration of countries thanks to a series of specialized world organizations, the central role played by the United Nations Security Council—all these things seemed pertinent and ready to function amid general approval. The major events of the following years, from German reunification to the Gulf War, seemed to confirm the viability of this organization. Seeing a legitimate order here was a double error of judgment on our part, which is still preventing us from working out a workable doctrine of the use of force.

Our first mistake lay in thinking that peace and war had become legal procedures. We thought that law would create order in the world, that is to say an organizational structure and authority over relations among countries. Even the British, usually pragmatic, allowed themselves to be seduced by this illusion. Their foreign minister actually wrote that he was fully anticipating "an imperial role for the United Nations."[45] This in the face of the fact that the international system embodied by the United Nations and similar institutions, including such military organizations as NATO, possesses no military strength of its own whatsoever.

Its capacity for order is all rhetoric; it has no hold over reality. From Somalia to Bosnia, each confrontation with the real world reveals more of the smoke and mirrors. Each confrontation shows that this "order" is not respected and has no means whatever of commanding respect. Each confrontation confirms that the instruments of force are and will remain in the hands of the States. To think of war and peace in legal terms runs counter to common sense, at best, whether we are talking about basic acts of power or about the limitations of the system that we invest with it.

For this is our second mistake. We fail to see that the very conception of this international system dooms it to powerlessness. This is not in fact a failure but the very nature of the system. An international system based on sovereignties *cannot* be a system with real power. Its founding principle stops it from being one, because it accepts from the start that decisions can only be made by general consensus, which is in itself a negation of the principle of authority. An organization such as this cannot generate a collective defense system. In responding to events it can only function through temporary or ad hoc coalitions, that is to say through acts of national sovereignty. Whether we look at NATO or at the Korean or Gulf Wars, the principle of the reality of force always wins out. Then too, a consensus agreement to take action—already mortally limiting—is not the same thing as action itself. Experience shows us that the disposition to pass resolutions is always stronger than the disposition to actually carry them out. The falsity of the international order is the flip side of the utopian legal system. In a system which believes that war and peace are legal actions, it is not surprising that many believe that a formal agreement to act can substitute for action itself.

A New Political Demand: Conformity

The international system's very structure robs it of all capacity to establish a permanent order. Every encounter with the real world reveals that the system's only power lies in the delegation of its symbolic authority. The dangerous ease with which new States are created and accepted aggravates this powerlessness further, since most of these new States are incredibly weak—nothing but phantoms dressed up in symbols. Furthermore, each new State dissolves the logic of sovereign power a little further in that of group membership.

We cannot conclude, however, that all this is artificial and that nothing has really changed. Over time, due to the prestige given to rhetoric, principles, and the law, the international system has *in fact* imposed a logic of group membership on the world. Declaration, apparent legal conformity, and formal endorsement of resolutions are now essentials. The system itself is powerless, but by creating sovereign States, it obtains the means to exercise power through them. To officially recognize a State is to grant it the power to be and to act.

That is the order of the international system: in the end it is an order of guilds. Just as there is an order among medical doctors, there is an order of States. In both cases, the order exercises none of the functions of its members; all it does is confer legitimacy on them. This power is basically that of registering or making official, and France—the country of notaries—should understand the importance of this better than any other country.

The use of force needs a seal of approval from now on. The foreign affairs of States must receive external approval, since force by itself no longer legitimizes anything. It is in this respect that the world order of today is no longer that of Metternich. What has changed is not the logic of power, but the logic of representation. The examples of the ostracized Burmese or Sudanese juntas, or of the detested Libyan, Serbian, or Iraqi dictator "Guides," illustrate this well, especially when compared to the sanctimonious prosperity enjoyed by their Syrian counterpart, who has understood that respect for appearances first conditions, then sets free the exercise of force.

The Temptation to Be Powerless

This type of system really tempts the world's powerful nations to become powerless. For them, foreign policy becomes an exercise with contradictory demands. On the one hand, having a clear doctrine to follow is essential for the exercise of force, because the political world has become more complex than ever before due to the increased number of both players and rules. More than ever, a State owes it to itself to define its own line of conduct. On the other hand, the sovereignty of States has become too restricted, even eroded, for a State to be able to legitimize itself; it needs to have legitimacy conferred upon it with an endorsement from an outside source. States are caught in the net of an international system that tolerates hypocrisy but not contempt. Acting as the arbiter of good manners, the media continually attack the actions of States. State leaders are thus forced to justify the basis of their good intentions to both national and international opinion, according to standards that are purely formal but indispensable just the same.

The temptation to be powerless begins with literal adherence to the utopian law. Relinquishing the exercise of power inevitably leads to powerlessness, because a scrupulous respect for the international system provides countless good reasons not to act. How many times France was told that it should not have intervened in Rwanda! For many great powers, this temptation is already very strong. Except in utmost emergencies, most great powers no longer make war at all. Nothing threatens them directly, and the use of force is a political choice that seems to be becoming rarer and rarer. All of these local, deadly wars where rabid paranoias tirelessly feed the slaughters don't really concern us, except if they were to spread to us . . . Who cares about Liberia or Sudan? It's not just that these wars seem nauseating or that we thought such savagery no longer occurred in our world; they are simply incomprehensible to us. Who are they fighting for in Liberia, in Sri Lanka, or in Afghanistan?

Thus at the very moment when the worthies are praising the creation of an international order based on law, others, just as worthy, see a permanent division of the world into the powerful and the barbarians. Some see in this a resurgence of the Roman-Medieval model, where zones of order and disorder were separated by buffer zones, once more brilliantly called *limes* (thresholds) in Latin. It is fashionable to recall the Middle Ages when we philosophize about the violence of our own times. True medievalists, who have been trying since the French historians Gustave Cohen and Marc Bloch to show that the Middle Ages were actually a time of enlightenment, will certainly appreciate the homage being paid to their ideas. Military historians will also appreciate this irony, since they know that the great massacres took place in the sixteenth and seventeenth centuries, which also produced the Renaissance, Descartes, and Racine.

It is interesting to look at those examples and see not only a profound ignorance of history but also a need to incorporate the present and the future into it. The real lesson of history is that conservatism in matters of doctrine is fatal. A superior doctrine is as often the reason for victory as superior forces. References to the past and reasoning by historical analogy are more irrelevant than ever, because the conditions for the use of force today are too new.

In particular, to legislate neutrality in policy is to yield to the temptation of another age, even if the utopian legal system gives us good excuses to do so. Such a policy leads to two obvious areas of contradiction.

The first contradiction concerns strategy. The geopolitics of the superpower dyad no longer exists; the purely political East–West axis has not been replaced by a North–South axis. The opposition of ideologies has not been replaced by the opposition of rich and poor. The switch over to the North–South paradigm is mostly on paper; most of the players are too tired to play. The same political reasoning and the same institutions remain in place, because—how amazing—the North and the West look alike on this odd world map. Thus, for example, NATO is miraculously well adapted to the role of world policeman, since its previous role was to combat the USSR. All you have to do is substitute the Oder-Neisse Line with the Thirtieth Parallel and, with just this limited adaptation, you find the same stakes and the same world order as before.

Such thinking makes our jaws drop. Binary geopolitics is a thing of the past. The end of the defensive alliances and the variety of the economic integrations make it impossible to think in either/or terms. The North and the South are everywhere these days; which is where depends on who is looking at them. Algeria may be a threat from the South to France, but for Mali it is a more affluent trading partner. In such cases we have to keep in mind the reality of the economic disparities in our world. In 1993, a Malian citizen had a purchasing power of $600 per year, while an Algerian had $4,600, and a French citizen $15,000. China could certainly be classified as a country of the South in its remote rural areas, but the per capita GNP of the average citizen of Shanghai in 1993 was as large as that of a resident of Tokyo in 1961. Was Japan, then, part of the South in 1961?

The very notion that there exists "one" empire or "one" North makes no sense. There is no more unanimity of policy in the North than in the South. Just as famine has never unified the poor countries, prosperity has not unified the wealthy ones. "The West" is not a valid strategic concept, because economic integration by itself does not bring about political order. Examination of one perfect instance of unification through prosperity—Southeast Asia—clearly shows that political unity has not followed. And when it comes to the three richest countries in the world, you have only to open a newspaper to see how real are the security conflicts that oppose the United States, for example, to Japan and also to Europe. But aren't these countries at least unified in their indifference to the others—the rest of the world? And who are these others, and who should be handling them? That Japan should let the United States handle Central America, that the United States in turn should let Russia handle the Caucasus, and that both expect Europe to handle the Maghreb—does all that really spring from a theory of organized indifference? If that's what it is, then the universality of this theory renders it quite useless to us. Unless, by this circuitous route, we come to see once again that the international system does not create order and that the only sources of real power are national ones . . .

The second contradiction concerns policy—that is, believing that neutrality is possible. In fact, it is no more possible than its opposite, the unilateral use of force. That is because there is no longer any such thing as "the outside world." When Jean-Christophe Ruffin writes that "Man is in the North; elsewhere there are only extras walking around in televised images,"[104] he underestimates the strength of those extras. The images are reality; their impact proves it. At any moment, the international media can make the most remote conflict into a priority that prevails over and dictates every government decision. Three weeks of horror-filled reports from Bosnia in the British media in the summer of 1992 blew away the British government's reluctance to commit itself in the Yugoslavian conflict. Two weeks of CNN coverage of Somalia in January 1993 persuaded the United States to intervene there, despite not wanting to at all. And later on similar images, this time showing losses and confusion among the American troops, were powerful enough to bring about their withdrawal.

Today the major States are as limited in their inability to act as they are in their ability to do so. The counterpart of the temptation to powerlessness is the temptation to activism. If the utopian system feeds the first, then the second is fueled by the illusion of humanitarian beneficence.

The Temptation of Sympathy

Humanitarian action cannot be sponsored by States. The natures of the two are antagonistic. The essence of humanitarian aid is its refusal to choose one distress over another. "How could one ever choose between good corpses and bad corpses?"[87]* Whatever its purpose, humanitarian activity can only be universal. "Humanitarian actions cannot be contained within borders." Its impartiality is not just a fragile defense, but the very principle underlying its legitimacy: "The victims, and only the victims, must be heard." Its true strength lies in is the purity of its motives; the constant efforts of all those who want to impute a bias to it prove this. Since humanitarianism has no self-interest, it tends to grow impatient with the system in place; its natural mode is "Let's do it right now!" This gives it a special aura. It also explains why so many humanitarian organizations feel tempted to convert the moral imperatives of individuals into collective political demands. This is a natural evolution; every moral cause tends to become a political program.

Because they are impelled by moral convictions, because their commitments come from their minds but their hearts are their only authority, the leaders of humanitarian causes believe that they are expressing universally held convictions. Their crusade is an invention, both a novelty and an expression of hidden desires. They are not just snipers—they are an advance party. They *know* that their enthusiasm is shared by others, or it will be. Today, polls confirm this to them and help to silence the skeptics. To defend human beings is to represent humanity. Spontaneously, when describing a project whose outcome was successful, Bernard Kouchner writes that "[C]ivil society won." A humanitarian commitment is a commitment on behalf of everyone. In fact, the "French Doctors"** are not just French people; they are the people of France.

---

*Unless otherwise noted, all quotations in this section are from Bernard Kouchner's *Le Malheur des autres* [*The Misfortunes of Others*], listing 87 in the Bibliography.

**A reference to Médecins sans Frontières/Doctors Without Borders, a humanitarian organization formerly headed by Bernard Kouchner. [Translator's note]

This conviction of being moral representatives creates a conviction of political legitimacy. Humanitarian action is no different from other large mass movements, such as anticolonialism. Both draw people together by appealing to their shared views and inner convictions. When confronted with deeply and widely held values, people forget their differences. They believe in a Republic of universal human convictions.

All these movements follow the same logic and share the same destiny: in the course of trying to turn themselves into policies, they become ideologies. Humanitarian action is not exempt.

How could it be otherwise? The defining quality of ideology is self-sufficiency, in the double meaning of autonomy and arrogance. Like other ideologies, humanitarianism instinctively distrusts the real world and its institutions. This is inevitable because those institutions have permitted, or even encouraged, the suffering that humanitarian action sets out to alleviate. Those institutions are necessarily at fault, especially the ones that pretend to address the same issues. The ideology on the rise thinks that "The Left and the Third-Worlders, who used to be important, chose their victims." To do that is a crime against the modern spirit, which does not understand such compromises or such allegiances.

The humanitarian ideology believes itself to be legitimate for at least two reasons. The first concerns territory, the second good intentions. The humanitarian aid worker, like the missionary and the militant Marxist before him, *knows* because he has *seen*. He expresses the innermost thoughts of everyone; he represents "civil society." Like other ideologies that have preceded it, humanitarian action transformed into ideology is convinced that it can finally establish a direct, living link between conviction and action. It can thus realize the ultimate activist dream: to go right past all the intermediaries and make each person an activist with the powers to match his convictions.

In theory as in actuality, humanitarianism is not unlike the other goodwill ideologies that preceded it or that still exist alongside it: we see the same certitude, the same self-sufficiency, the same ambition. Like other ideologies, it believes itself to be more just, more direct, and more humane than those it is replacing. "Humanitarian intervention will be the cement of world peace," writes Bernard Kouchner, who confidently concludes: "A world consciousness is forming that will eventually lead to a world government." Saint Augustine had the same conception of the Church, and Karl Marx of the workers' movement. Bernard Kouchner agrees with this when he writes, "We invented the humanitarian movement because the world needed it to replace Marxism." The logic of ideologies is, by nature, the logic of being "the first to . . . ."

Although humanitarian action can easily drift into ideology, its very nature prevents it from becoming official State policy. Humanitarianism is impelled by "*other* people's misfortunes," whereas it is the interest of the State's *own* citizens that guides its official policy. The latter are as unchanging as the former are diverse. The goal of State policy, and of the doctrine behind it, is to serve its own interests as well as it can at the expense of, even in conflict with, interests lying outside that State. In many ways, the relationship of the State to humanitarianism is similar to its relationship to the military. Both relationships are motivated by "practical" considerations involving territorial goals. The territory of the first is the field of helping others; the territory of the second is the field of defeating others. Left to their natural devices, both the military and the humanitarians will pursue their respective actions until they attain their goals. For both the military and the humanitarians, it is the State that must set limits both on their goals and on their means of attaining them—organizations do not dictate such matters to States. This subordination is the very essence of political power.

Partiality is necessary for a strategy of force to succeed, but it will cause a humanitarian project to fail. Humanitarianism is non-governmental by nature, not by default. Its legitimacy derives from the distress of each and not from the interests of a collectivity, as the State's actions do. Humanitarian action is not a policy; it is a spiritual need. The living force of humanitarianism is the direct personal link between the suffering of one person and another person's awareness of it. It's a pure affair of the heart. As the French film star Simone Signoret used to say so well, "We receive neither orders nor instructions. We just feel it in our hearts."

Humanitarian intervention is carried out on a purely emotional basis, with all that that implies as to both its intensity and its partiality. Kurds, Bosnians, and Rwandans have all benefited from its passion. On the other hand, the Sudanese, Angolans, Azeris, and other Tadjiks are all free to cut each other's throats without anyone getting in their way. We have no idea why, but their fate is of little interest to the public. In such cases, no doubt, "humanitarian politics" would insist that they be helped anyway. "We have to be able to intervene wherever we are called."

We had better hope that this philosophy does not become official State policy, because it has already been interpreted in dubious ways. The Chinese called their intervention in Tibet in 1950 "humanitarian," as did the Soviets in Afghanistan in 1979, the Syrians in Lebanon in 1987, the Russians in Georgia in 1993, and so forth. The original calls for help were not always faked—by no means. But they nearly always turned out badly for the callers, because the community of States is not a civil society. A mission undertaken for the public good makes sense within the boundaries of a country, because there is a State in place that represents the general good and whose authority can prevail over competing interests. But no such agreement exists *between* States. That is why breaches of sovereignty have such unforeseen and often calamitous consequences.

To give sovereign power to one State over another—or to tolerate this—can only be acceptable in the presence of a superior authority—which does not exist. To pretend that such an authority exists, or will ever exist, on the strength of the politics of a *fait accompli* is not only naive, it is also an encouragement to commit crimes in the name of this fiction.

Humanitarian organizations possess an enthusiasm, a sincerity, and a remarkable freedom to represent only themselves that enables them to do things that would destroy States, with their delicate balancing acts. Well paid only in daily bravery, the French Doctors, for example, are able to choose their battles and to act at once upon their choices. Not to function in this way would go against the basic nature of their organization, just as it would go against the basic nature of a State to function as the Doctors do. Because humanitarian action defines itself as universal, it excludes the two fundamental characteristics of a State's foreign policy: the sense of time as a factor, and discerning where its interests lie. This leads to splendid actions as well as to disasters. "We supported our Afghan friends, the proud and free mountain warriors, but we opposed the extremists," boasted Bernard Kouchner. Could he distinguish between the two today? The Pashtoons, who so courageously fought the Soviets, are today building themselves a new nation by means of ethnic cleansing. Are they any less fanatical than the Islamic fundamentalists who are devastating Kabul?

No one would hold it against a physician that he treats all comers, yet the average citizen is guilty of wanting us to believe that the Hippocratic oath is a political program. The suffering or the approaching death of a man purifies the soul of both the sufferer and the witnesses. Confronted by the universal and immemorial enemies of mankind, we feel the ultimate solidarity of our species. But what is true for each individual is not necessarily true for all people together.

Organizations and countries are not simply aggregations of individuals. Failing to understand this is the fundamental mistake of both the humanitarian ideology and the utopian legal system. Both are utopias of the civil society and both believe that they can establish a global civil society. It is no accident that they share the conviction that universal principles of law or ethics can be proclaimed and that they already lie dormant in the breast of every human being. The fusion of these two utopias in the concept of a "law of intervention" shows both the idealism and the contradiction of this phrase, which laughs off its own illogic.

Humanitarian Logic, War Logic?

These utopias commit a fundamental error of judgment. They refuse to accept the logic of the force-based relations that exist between sovereign States and fail to see that they are the foundation of everything else; there is no other system. Certain death was, briefly, the common borderline of all States. The utopias find it very abrasive to come into contact with the real world. From Somalia to Cambodia and Bosnia, the increasing number of failures of policies based on humanitarianism are showing us just how brutal are the consequences of this abrasion. In the meantime, however, the political consequences are grave: the sentimental promotion of these nonsensical policies is eroding the legitimacy of States. These utopias thus are contributing to the very instabilities that they claim to be counteracting. And, more important, they are radicalizing war.

International law, in its utopian way, preaches that war and peace are legal processes. Actually, in a way, war is the pursuit of the law by other means. Humanitarian ideology shares this profound misunderstanding of the logic of power and ends up with some surprising contradictions. The utopian voice of civil society begins by announcing that war is being progressively eradicated. This is presented as an inevitable result of the movement set in motion by the law of intervention. It is not a wish, it is a theorem: "The danger of the war of all against all is slowly giving way to a social contract on a global scale."[87] Why? Because "intervention will limit or prevent wars." At the very least the illegal wars between States. But other crusades await them.

More than most people, Bernard Kouchner has seen murderous insanity touch his loved ones and deny, by death, the evangelization of democracy. In the eyes of the humanitarian ideology, an attitude like his rises above politics because, by definition, there is nothing more universally human than humanitarianism. Like the Catholic ideology in its time, humanitarianism claims to be monolithic—it encompasses all of mankind. To reject it, to kill its missionaries, would be an act not only of aggression but of spiritual excommunication. It would be tantamount to declaring that one is inhuman, thus opening oneself to every kind of violence. At this stage, writes Bernard Kouchner, "[W]e're getting to the point where intervention stops and the war of civilizations begins."

Yet the civilization that he defends is that of everyone, not just in the West. Like Catholicism, humanitarianism finds such reductionism deeply offensive; it is convinced that its message dwells in the heart of every person. This claim is the very foundation of the utopian vision of the universal civil society.

This war of civilization must therefore be a radical one. It is a combat between day and night, between the physician and death. This is not the face-off of two relativisms; it is the irreducible opposition of two absolute moralities. If Napoleon was Robespierre on horseback, Bernard Kouchner is Saint-Just in a helicopter.

Such an attitude has serious consequences. The defense of mankind leads finally to a more radical conception of war than the logics of force, which are influenced by a sense of relativity and equilibrium. This paradox is common to all ideologies of human happiness; their certainties make their logics extremely rigid. For them, there can only be wars of civilization against the barbarians. The logic of the Holy War is one such—it is the logic of the end of history.

Some people believe in the end of history and believe that it is not far off. Beneath the monumental disruptions that have piled up since 1989, they see the forces of the civil society in the process of shaping the world. "The farce of the Soviet *Putsch* proves this absolutely," says Bernard Kouchner. Such a summation is stupefying. For anyone who saw it up close, the failure of this *Putsch* was due entirely to the carelessness of its leaders and owed nothing to world opinion. The world fears the instability of such a powerful State so much that no country would have opposed the *Putsch;* in fact, many States would have made their peace with a new Brezhnev-style regime in the Soviet Union. After Tienanmen Square, all of China's neighbors expressed their condolences—in the Asian sense of the word, that is to say by reassuring China that she still belonged to their community. It is not just a hunger for trade that makes China's neighbors so cautious, but also an acute sense of her fragility and the memory of the disaster that was China in chaos. We only read events well from a distance. History has taught China's neighbors the hard way that the best they can hope for is for China to remain united and on her own territory; usually the two go together.

Unity and stability are the two preconditions for the evolution of States. Once secure, they can become more amenable to change. To continue using China as an example, the Tibetan independence movement was never so successful as between 1986 and 1988, when Beijing thought that it had reconciled the prosperity of its society with the stability of its regime. Some restrictions were eased, but these openings have since been hermetically sealed off again with pitiless repression. There is no resignation among the Tibetans, just a sense of the slow passage of time as experienced by States, so different from the urgency of humanitarian organizations. To confuse the two is a sin of the intellect against reality, all the more easily committed because it affects only others. To campaign in favor of sending arms into the Bosnian furnace is of no consequence in Washington or Paris. The demand for a "law of intervention," and the thoughtlessness of those requesting it (few of whom are as brave as Bernard Kouchner) show, at best, an incredible shallowness.

For the erosion of the legitimacy of States and the radicalization of war make a volatile mixture. To denounce the illegitimacy of a fragile State by addressing its population contributes to breaking it up into antagonistic groups. It results in civil war and the radicalization of States. States attempt to stop the national deterioration by mobilizing the people against a foreign enemy, in the name of a war for civilization that becomes a self-fulfilling prophecy. The alliance of the humanitarian and the legal utopias accelerates this downward spiral by holding out the enticement of sovereign independence to each of these warring groups, regardless of their capacity to handle this responsibility. The former Yugoslavia and Central Asia are perfect examples of the devastating power of these mechanisms. "I never wanted *that*," said Admiral Horthy in 1945, after Hungary's commitment to the Axis powers had ended in disaster.

A Strategic Doctrine Must Incorporate the Media

Deadly good intentions are nothing new, but the media now provide them with ways of bypassing the States. In the process, the media transform the exercise of power. We must think about taking the media into account in the conception and application of a strategic doctrine. From now on, the media will be able to organize, according to their biases, a direct democracy of the intolerable. Born from the sorrows of people elsewhere, the humanitarian ideology flourishes on guilt at home. It can call on governments every day to justify themselves on television news programs. The *Tribune* becomes a tribunal. The meeting of French politicians called by the sponsors of the "For Sarajevo" list during the European elections laid bare this perversion of function. The meeting somewhat resembled the self-criticism sessions of the Chinese Cultural Revolution; both its spirit and its violence were quite similar. The democratic virtue of such a process is doubtful. It is sad that we've reached the point where elected officials feel they have to justify themselves to self-proclaimed representatives of public opinion.

Humanitarian ideology and the media are fueled by the same logic of emotionalism. If everyone does not share the feeling they are trying to tap, then that feeling is not worth much. "Without pictures, no indignation," admits Bernard Kouchner, who also knows that the emotionalism of the media has its limits. These surges of feeling are fleeting; they last "two weeks on average." This is because wall-to-wall media coverage quickly makes people indifferent and annoyed. Just ask those who are still trying to drum up public interest in Cambodia or Rwanda. Repeated restatement of a problem in the media leads people to believe that nothing can be done to remedy it, since the problem is still there. The patient, deliberate pace of most conflict resolution doesn't march very well with the mercurial instability of the media. It is interesting to ask oneself what policies, what future a State could build for itself, if it too had to change its priorities every two weeks. Can we believe that the building of France would have held TV viewers' attention week after week for ten centuries?

The interest of the media not only dries up quickly; it only catches fire when it is fueled by prejudices. The fate of the Kurds moves the hearts of Europeans, but it does no such thing for their Mideastern neighbors, who feel about as much affection for the Kurds as the French did for the Vikings who pillaged them in the eleventh century, and for the same reasons. The Kurds are considered masterful thieves and pitiless fighters. Similarly, the description of day-to-day events in Bosnia often owes more to the imaginings of certain journalists and intellectuals than to the facts. The stupefyingly large gap between reality and its portrayal in the media seems not to bother anyone, so much are the media becoming the reality. In the fall of 1994, for example, the Serbian attack on Bihac was described as a supplementary carnage, accompanied by a new assault on Sarajevo, where the inhabitants had again taken refuge in their basements. The military present on the ground, however, painted a completely different picture. In both places the Serbs' aggression had been calibrated to produce the most disarray with the fewest possible casualties among the population. Two-thirds of the patients who were in the hospital in Bihac at the beginning of December were already there before the Serbian offensive. The assailants showed no humane concern at all, only great skill in manipulating the media.

At the time in Sarajevo, most of the firepower was concentrated on the press headquarters. In Bihac, the Serbs proclaimed their resolve to end all resistance against them. But they were careful not to occupy the city and they left a corridor open to the north. By doing so, they won on two levels. On the one hand they knew that their mobility and knowledge of the terrain would limit reactions by the UN and the foreign States, who were being kept informed by their military. On the other hand, the Serbs knew they could count on the aroused indignation of the media to inflate both their exploits and the image of their determination. They knew that world opinion would hate them all the more but also that the same world opinion would be still more reluctant to commit their troops against them. The way the United States backed off proved the effectiveness of this policy. The media thus became the unwitting accomplice of the Serbian strategy.

We must reexamine how we implement our foreign policy. The media are calling into question not our policies on the use of force but how they are carried out. The grip of the media will not be broken by the practice of lying to them and then confusing those lies with legitimate secrecy. The legitimacy of real secrecy will only be destroyed. States will achieve nothing by trying to outwit the media at their own game of emotions and bulletins; they will only lose their credibility and their maneuvering room. But by holding fast—no matter what—to a few fundamental principles they will regain authority over the system. This continuity is the privilege of States, and it is a true force when dealing with the instability of the media. Our leaders will need a thought-out, coherent vision of the interests at stake. The media is like a watchdog: it smells fear or weakness, and grows more aggressive in response.

The use of force is thus thrown back on its primary imperative: the need for a doctrine. Indeed, such a doctrine is not just required for military effectiveness; it is a basic element of the foreign policies of States. Without such a doctrine in place, States will have their foreign policies forced upon them by the unpredictable movements of mass emotions. In the past, the lack of a doctrine exposed a great power to the risk of being unable to act; today, it exposes a State to the risk of being forced to act—perhaps against its own interests.

For France, such a necessity represents a radical change. Indeed, the doctrine France needs is no longer a simple doctine of defense. If we look at the historical record carefully, France's strategic doctrine has always been formulated in response to aggressions—and it is still so today. This illustrates less the pacifist character of France than the essentially military nature of its doctrine. Our national security will be less and less exclusively military and defensive. We French need a strategic doctrine that is based on positive objectives as well.

CHAPTER 11

Foundations

We need a new political science for a new world.

—Alexis de Tocqueville

The Rosy Future of War

This world is without precedent. It is as different from the Cold War as it is from the Middle Ages, so the past offers no basis for comparison. The planet continues to become more and more unified and at the same time more and more fragmented, and the distinction between war and peace is getting lost. There are no more world wars, but instead we have local wars, which have increased in cruelty and multiplied to record numbers. Nothing threatens France any longer, yet France has never before deployed so many troops outside her borders. Legal and economic integrations keep on growing, but they are powerless to keep the peace, because war cannot be stopped by wealth or by laws. These grandiose dreams of integration are an answer to yesterday's wars, which were wars of conquest and domination. How many times have the opponents of building an integrated Europe been told that this was the best way to stabilize Germany? But tomorrow's wars will not result from the ambitions of States, rather from their weaknesses. Not having taken this into account, the principles and the rules of the system of international law, far from preventing war, will make sure that war has a rosy future.

The vulnerability and the instability of States will be the main causes of war in the future, and the international system as it stands has no solution to offer. Its generous utopias have no meaning in countries ruled by fear of the future. The system can only wring its hands and deplore such wars; sometimes it actually contributes to them by casually permitting the creation of so many weak new States. But it does worse. By obstinately clinging to the utopian concept of a world society of equal States, it prevents the few States capable of wielding real power from committing it in effective ways. Only the interventions of strong States could really contain the new wars. The main world powers all possess the military power needed to successfully intervene in such crises, while themselves incurring only limited risks. But, having learned from recent experiences, in the future these powerful states will commit themselves only on condition of retaining operational control. The international organizations, however, are not ready to hand this control over to these world powers, because that would wreck the pretense of a world consensus, which alone gives them the illusion of legitimacy. Moreover, these same world powers are the only ones in a position to offer any warring States any credible alternatives to war; only they have enough money and influence to do it.

In either case, the great States themselves must be willing to act. The least one can say is that they are not exactly receiving encouragement. On the contrary, they are being weighed down by the vanity, inertia and suspicion of the international system, combined with the wariness of their public opinion and of many of their leaders as well. Their own vital interests are rarely affected by these multiplying conflicts; indifference is usually cheaper for them than intervention. By fostering inaction to such an extent, the international system destroys its own ambitions. For the lack of interest of the great powers leaves the field open to the troublemakers. They are guaranteed impunity, as well as the assurance that the strongest of them will win out: the governments in Syria and Iran, terrorists only yesterday, as well as the imperialistic Serbia of today illustrate this clearly. By ignoring the realities of force, the utopian legal system allows its most brutal forms to prevail.

The Great Powers Are United in Reluctance

The immobilization of the principal States has already reached the point of irreversibility. A quick look at France's permanent, actual, or potential partners at the United Nations Security Council spotlights the truth of this.

The two prime candidates for Council membership, Japan and Germany, are two archetypes of this culture of reluctance. We have already considered the case of Japan: any Japanese commitment overseas brings down the unanimous hostility of its neighbors and of its own citizenry. Germany's situation is rather similar. In 1993, 72 percent of Germans opposed any participation in NATO's military peacekeeping efforts. An even greater percentage (82 percent) opposed taking part in such actions under the United Nations.[59] During a 1993 poll, of the six issues judged most important by at least half of all Germans, only one—Yugoslavia—involved foreign policy. When answering specific questions regarding foreign policy, German public opinion reveals support only for the smoother integration of Germany into the European community and for the stability of Germany's neighbors.

Unfortunately, these two recruits will not differ greatly from most of the present permanent members of the Security Council. China has never intervened in foreign affairs on the side of peace. Its only foreign involvements with its neighbors have been hostile: wars with India and Vietnam, armed standoffs with Taiwan and the Soviet Union, military activity in the China Sea, etc. China is the extreme case of strategic selfishness.

The United Kingdom long ago gave up on foreign interventions except when its own interests are at stake or the United States asks it for help. It only reluctantly committed itself in

Bosnia under intense public pressure; this is the only recent exception to its rule of strict abstinence. The United Kingdom has deemed that foreign intervention is useful only when it is massive in scale and when its goals are precise and realistic. Experience shows that this is very rare.

Russia is an even more revealing case. She has abdicated all responsibility, even at the regional level, while still defending her own interests as strongly as ever. *The* priority in her foreign policy is the stabilization of her immediate neighbors, that is to say the non-Russian republics of the former Soviet Union. The idea is to surround Russia with secure territory on all her defensible borders. Russia will not accept any opposition to this policy; there are over 120,000 Red Army troops on active duty in these territories. These troops are often involved in major operations whose only purpose is to maintain order in Russia's immediate environs.

But Russia wants to control without having to govern. Russia does not want to reconstitute an empire where she would be responsible for its former republics, which are often in chaos. She only plays the Russian nationalist card in a tactical way. She only defends Russian minorities when her own interests are at stake, as they are in the Baltic states and Moldova, and has likewise supported pro-Russian parties only when it has suited her, as in Azerbaijan and in Ukraine. Russia is not following any russification policy, even though language, history, and administration are the bulwarks of any nationalism.

The same is true of the border regions *within* present-day Russia. These regions have always been crucial to the security and prosperity of the Russian heartland. They have never known a policy of true integration, only an uncaring rule. The Chechen crisis is one of the numerous, predictable results of this policy. Chechnya is an interior rampart; beyond it lies the "near abroad" of the republics of the Caucasus; together these isolate Russia from the Turkish and Iranian threats. Chechnya also represents an important economic zone—a declining one—due to its rich petroleum deposits and the industries related to them. Like the Caucasian republics themselves and like Eastern Siberia, Chechnya is both a source of wealth and a buffer territory.

Russia's policy toward these territories has remained consistent for centuries. These territories constitute the living dermis, or inner skin, of Russia; the "near abroad" States are her epidermis. The stability of each one of these territories is a Russian vital interest. Within the strict limits of the interests of Russia alone, it is indispensable for her to assure complete, unfailing control over them; any exception whatever would set a mortally dangerous precedent. The local or regional effects of this policy are unintended but deadly. As Olivier Roy has commented, the only certain effect of such a policy is to work against the stability of these States and to distance their elites from Russia. This promises some difficult times in Russia's future.

The United States, or Reluctance as Uncertainty

The United States has followed the same fear-of-commitment policy as the other great powers. Its interventions in Panama or Haiti are less significant than its withdrawal from Europe and Asia. This has made the United States clearly less of a factor on the world scene since the end of the Cold War. For the first time the United States is not entirely in control of its own agenda and no longer has the option of isolationism. It can neither take up a marginal position in the world nor remain in the center of the world stage under conditions dictated by others. It has never known this double bind, which is the common lot of other countries. Learning how to handle this common dilemma will be a long and difficult process filled with false starts, which will reduce for a long time to come its willingness to get involved on the world stage.

The United States remains unarguably the most powerful nation in the world. But it is now among peers. Whether we look at the United Nations, the OSCE, APEC, NAFTA or any of the other regional agreements that have popped up of late, multilateral agreements are slowly tying up American leadership. To what extent will the United States be willing to follow the laws imposed by such multilateral agreements? Recent major negotiations show an extreme reluctance to do so on the part of the Americans. They accepted an international commercial jurisdiction only under the condition that they reserve the right to be free of it at will. When the convention prohibiting chemical weapons was being drawn up, the United States found itself closest to the most offending countries in refusing to submit to surprise inspections. Under the "Open Skies" treaty, which authorizes mutual surveillance flights, the United States has refused others this right. In international peacekeeping operations, American troops may never come under the command of foreign officers. The United States is also the only country not to sign the biodiversity convention, which guarantees protection to endangered species, because it sees the convention as too "intrusive." The list is interminably long and diverse enough to be convincing. These refusals to submit to outside authority are not just wounded vanity on the part of the United States. They are also a reflection of two of the basic elements of American politics: the absolute need to be on top and the conviction that its beliefs are universal.

Superiority—being on top—is a latent and immutable given of American society because that society is based on a culture of confrontation. From its earliest beginnings to World War II, the United States has traveled through history like a cowboy on horseback through a Western. Its conception of foreign relations—from the Native Americans to the Axis Powers—is that of antagonistic relations where superior force wins in the end. The Cold War elaborated this philosophy in its own way. For the first time, the very existence of the United States was seriously threatened. For the Americans, the launch of the Sputnik satellite and the development of the first Soviet thermonuclear weapon were primarily not humiliations, but scares: once the Red(skins) had gotten hold of rifles, now the Reds had gotten hold of missiles and bombs. The confrontation with the Soviets was rightly experienced as an archetype: the feeling of superiority here crossed over from the cultural—"We are better than the Indians"—to the strategic—"We are stronger than the Soviets."

A culture like America's does not exclude rallying together and mass mobilization. It includes higher values that demand total commitment. The concept of higher ideals that are worth fighting to the death for is very important to American culture. It is at once the common dream of its Founding Fathers and the glue, constantly renewed, that holds together the many elements of the melting pot. This reality is highly emotional and deeply anchored in the American heart: we underestimate it in Europe. We tend to assume that Americans feel the same and think the same as we do about the use of force. But their political culture is steeped in the logic of superiority; it easily resorts to violence but it is not cynical or calculating. The cold and deliberate use of force, using resources and people for the purposes of the State, plays no part in the political culture of the United States.

The only U.S. politicians to have made their names with such practices were both Europeans; both were advisors, never elected to office. Kissinger and Brzezinsky are both marginal to American politics. Even today, America's use of force remains tied to the defense of certain values. The colossal hypocrisy that this permits in American political life should not make us discount these values, which are so strong that their invocation alone justifies the ultimate sacrifice of American lives. The attempts of Jimmy Carter and Bill Clinton to explain this moral legitimacy to us bring both smiles and consternation to our faces, but for Americans they represent a reality that often overrules reasons of State. Thus we recently watched, astonished, as an advisor to Bill Clinton, wishing to protest Muslim fundamentalism, abruptly ended an official visit to Central Asia because two imams had been condemned without due process . . .

The Cold War was a conflict over values and dreams, those of Lenin and Stalin against those of Washington and Jefferson. The exact correlation between America's cultural values and the demands of its geopolitics was only an interlude—which has ended.

From now on, no more combat over values. Some values have become universalized and are no longer just American values; other values remain American and are not universally accepted. Already in 1956 George Kennan noted that the United States' tendency to believe in the universal nature of its own value system would inevitably be a source of serious misunderstanding and trouble.[85] This misunderstanding manifests itself today in the increasing difficulty that American political leaders experience when trying to convince their public of the need for a proactive foreign policy when there are no major American interests to defend. And a simple use of force somewhere is not enough of an issue to mobilize the American public. President Bush lost by a wide margin in 1992 in spite of his exceptional success as a world leader. His successor was elected on a platform of "America first," but as time goes on it is clear that he cannot make the United States walk away from its international responsibilities.

The United States is no longer leading the process of international integration, but rather is confronting it. Its ability to bring order to the new geopolitics is limited by its reluctance to accept the consequences of leadership. And this dilemma will burden the Americans for a long time to come with delays and contradictory decisions. The United States wants to lead without committing fully to leadership: at the United Nations it orders world politics without taking part in them; in Asia it serves as a regional arbiter without ever actually intervening; in the GATT talks it preached an end to commercial independence yet seeks to protects its own interests; in NATO, the United States alone guarantees the security of the members, yet it will no longer define the guarantees. On each new stage, the dilemmas facing American power are multiplying. With each new performance, America's distaste for international commitment increases.

Isolationism and Crises

The major powers have hesitated to commit themselves in foreign conflicts, but they have not compensated by maintaining solid strategic alliances. These alliances have come unraveled by the same unilateral process as the major ones. In Asia as in Europe, the United States has not given up its leadership, but it would like to choose the consequences of its involvement. It has reduced its military presence, but has not in any way comparably reduced its political ambitions. The American attitude towards its allies is in fact similar to that of Russia towards the "near abroad." Both want to control without having either to manage or to commit.

The unraveling of alliances, the reluctance to commit, and the powerlessness of international organizations make any solidarity uncertain at best. Take Bosnia as an example. The Irish couldn't intervene because they're neutral, the Italians because the Bosnians are historic enemies, the Greeks because Bosnia is a neighboring state, the Germans because they are the Germans—they are forbidden to intervene anywhere. Tomorrow when a crisis breaks out, what solidarity will there be? On what basis? It is no accident that France alone intervened in Rwanda and was criticized for doing so, in spite of the fact that the States of Europe are committed to acting together. If France were obliged to involve itself more directly in the Algerian crisis, for example, what backing could it hope for? The only United Nations troops remaining in Somalia or in Cambodia are mercenaries from poor countries for whom such missions are a boon. Solidarity between States is a delicate house-plant; it travels badly from the conference room to the battlefield. Together with the nervous weakness of the international legal system, this naturally leads to complete avoidance of foreign commitments, except in life-or-death emergencies like Kuwait or domestic political necessity, like the U.S. intervention in Haiti.

In the future, responsibility in foreign affairs will be decided on a case-by-case basis, without any previous collective commitment. Such a choice will always be difficult. It will disrupt the logic of collective thinking and its comfortable and convenient passivity. It may well look arrogant. François Mitterrand learned this lesson at Sarajevo.

The Real Stakes: The Stability of States

Can peace be guaranteed? Clearly not. The economic and legal integration of countries will not bring about a stable political order. The international system is not designed to deal with the main reason for war, which is the weakness of a growing number of States. The great powers are more and more hesitant to make commitments to resolve crises that do not directly concern them.

This does not mean that they are indifferent. Between unconditional intervention in any and every crisis, as demanded by someone like Bernard Kouchner, and completely ignoring them all, as Jean-Christophe Ruffin suggests, there is an effective way to avoid wars. This consists in giving absolute priority to the stability of States. For such stability is the precondition—the *sine qua non*— for any peace, because the instability of States is the primary source of war. Close examination of two centuries of conflicts reveals that totalitarian states are no more likely to start a war than are democracies. In unstable States, however, the probability of war *doubles*.[105] Periods of transition to a democratic system are particularly unstable.[92] At such times, the power-wielding classes, who are losing ground, are apt to incite the masses with nationalism and the threat of outside aggression so as to retain their power. Such a process led Germany to start World War I and Japan to invade Manchuria. It plays an important role in the Russian war in Chechnya and the Serbian war in Bosnia. This conversion of State instability into war can come about for other reasons besides a once-dominant State feeling threatened. The transition to democracy unleashes many forces that can easily generate conflicts: fear of revolt (Russia today, China tomorrow?), fear of being denied one's due (the Serbs, the Kurds), the appearance of radical ideologies (Muslim fundamentalism), and so forth.

Apart from peace, development and democracy can only develop in stable States. There exists no example of a State whose prosperity or whose justice came into being under conditions of instability. But examples of unstable States that have lost those virtues abound. Historical logic seems to be a one-way street. Economic development necessarily brings human rights along behind it. From Brazil to Korea via Spain, this process is sometimes slow but it is inescapable. On the other hand, human rights cannot survive misery and the prosperity of nations cannot survive the instability of States.

Our main objective, then, should be stability, not democracy. We should stop reveling in the creation of hopes and movements when we are not committed to accepting responsibility for them. We should not be taken in by our own rhetoric. That our vision of human rights has been endorsed and ratified as the official moral stance of a new international order is a formidable windfall of power. We must use that power sparingly and lucidly.

The ceaseless promotion of our own values as universal and unique can only do us harm. Weak or poor countries will inevitably ask us to pay for the changes that we have encouraged them to make. It has become clear that we don't want to pick up the tab for democracy and also that the utopian legal system is incapable of doing so; it's nothing but a splendid verbal illusion. The strong countries will firmly reject this moral colonialism. At the least, we risk triggering the rejection of just what we want to support. At the worst, we may actually cause the strengthening of values diametrically opposed to our own, as is currently happening in Asia. An internal memo at the U.S. State Department recently listed the growing opposition among America's principal allies to its promotion of so-called "universal values." The list is instructive: conflict with Singapore (over corporal punishment), with Indonesia (over labor laws), with China (over human rights), and with Thailand (over corruption). In each case the Asian countries have followed their own beliefs.

When the stability of States is assured and their economic development is well under way, then promoting democracy becomes a credible goal. There is no reason to tolerate the Libyan or Burmese juntas. Countries like the Philippines and Burkina Faso, which are risking the democratic experiment without becoming prosperous, should qualify for our special support. But this choice is ultimately theirs and not ours; we should not impose it on them. Human rights constitute a moral ambition, not a foreign policy. To give up on human rights would be to abdicate our very humanity; to try to obtain them by preaching morality betrays the expectations of those who are counting on our help. Our policies must focus on essentials. Rather than sentimentally promoting some unrealizable utopia, we should work toward establishing the essential foundation of all development of justice and prosperity: the stability of the State.

This is obviously a more modest goal, and less emotionally satisfying. Such a goal means working with governments that we find reprehensible and seeming at times to agree to, if not actually to support, their actions. But the history of the past thirty years has shown us that only stable States have been able to shake off the authoritarian regimes they started out with. From the Soviet Union to Latin America, not to mention the paradoxes of China, the proof is irrefutable. But it requires inexhaustible patience . . .

The Cold War taught the world only one lesson that will outlive it, and that is that the logic of détente works. The USSR would have waged war, and nuclear war at that. But she didn't do it, because she had other options. Beginning in 1972, the institutionalization of détente started the erosion of the Soviet Union—because the chains of war no longer held its empire together. Today's détente is the stability of States.

Giving priority to stability does not constitute a blank check. On the contrary, it is an effective way to ensure the legitimacy of States. Those attributes of a State are absolutely linked together; there can be no stability without legitimacy, or vice versa. But stability must come first. It will not last without legitimacy, but it is necessary for the establishment of legitimacy. This is our true goal. We don't need to prescribe some magical formula dictating just what this legitimate State must be, but we must insist that it be one.

Stability does not require a policy of immobility; on the contrary, it is the precondition for moving forward. Only once States have been assured of their permanence can they envisage making deep structural changes, especially if those changes are being pushed by outsiders. That authoritarian regimes need stability is obvious— they naturally suspect that we want them to collapse. But democracies need it too. Note the misgivings of the smaller States about the growth of European unification. Their strong reaction in early 1995 to the proposal to reduce the number of working languages used by the Commission is a good example. The idea was to reduce the number of languages used on a daily basis to the five principal ones. These five languages are those spoken by 85 percent of the population of the European Union and already are, for all practical purposes, the only ones used at the Commission on a day-to-day basis. The objection of the small States is symbolic, because they always feel threatened by dilution. The Belgian press, for example, declared that "such a reform would destroy Belgium."[31]

The original goal of détente was to reduce fear, not to make concessions, still less to make political accommodations. Today, fear is once again a major force owing to the splintering of nations into groups whose insecurities are growing as their sizes are shrinking.

The best ways to combat these fears is to practice transparency and to insist that existing States continue to act in concert.

Transparency, or laying one's cards on the table, is a major innovation that needs to be generalized by every possible means because it allays suspicions. It is because the United States was able to fully inform both India and Pakistan about each other's military preparations in 1989 that it was able to convince both countries not to drift into war—which would undoubtedly have been nuclear. Similarly, the strict mutual-verification clauses built into recent disarmament treaties are the only assurance of their credibility. We should make the extension into other domains of mutual surveillance treaties, like the "Open Skies" treaty, a priority in our security policies. For peace is our first responsibility, both within and between nations. The future wars that will interrupt such peace will most often result from fear, hate, or dread of what tomorrow may bring. Neither international law nor the market economy will overcome this. Our responsibility is not to promote the illusion of universal values, but rather to create political mechanisms that can support this stability and allay these fears.

The stabilization of States assumes avoiding both their breakup and their multiplication. New States should only be recognized with extreme caution. Since these new States are the result of internal rifts that have turned one part of a nation against another, they are most likely cauldrons of instability. Furthermore, their small size makes their economic future problematic. In every Eastern European state, 1994 saw protest votes for the ousted Communist parties markedly increase. These votes are a sign not of nostalgia for the past, but rather of the difficulties that have accompanied the changes there— which, meanwhile, have been remarkably successful. We ought to be very concerned about the future of these little divided-up States and the various instabilities that the failure of their independent economic developments will bring about. To accept the unlimited creation of newer, smaller States in the name of the utopian legal system, then, is to fail in our primary responsibility, which is to promote prosperity and peace. Our duty and our best interests lie in helping these populations to live with one another rather than to support their separating. We must also encourage neighboring small States to cooperate with one another.

The European Union has the power to do much good in this area. When the negotiations start concerning the Baltic States joining the European Union, should we not begin to think about opening a discussion of linking these three States together as a prerequisite to their entrance into the Union? Their combined population is equal to that of Austria (8,000,000), while their GNP is twenty times smaller. Even combined together, their chances for successful economic development are poor. As separate States, they are zero. We will pay the economic and political consequences if we do not make the stability and unity of States a priority. The bill for failing to do so may be more than we can afford. Yugoslavia is a hard lesson for us. What will happen tomorrow in the Baltic States or in Slovakia? Would the latter have separated from the Czechs had Europe agreed in time to help modernize Slovakia and invest in its economic stability? The Czechs have given in to the illusion that they can emulate Germany, while the Slovaks are pursuing the illusion of independence. Their failure is ours too. Are we not also preparing the same fate for Ukraine by ignoring its poorer, more distant, Russified eastern half while investing in its wealthier, more Europeanized western half?

An Essential Precondition:
Assuring the Stability of Europe

How can the stability we need come to prevail in Europe? The European Union is already a first step in this direction, a stable example to all neighboring States. But to go one step further and assure these neighbors' stability, the European Union must be on an equal footing with the United States. The trans-Atlantic relationship must be balanced before Central Europe can be integrated. Let us be realistic: Russia will never allow its former sphere of influence to become the "near abroad" of the United States in Europe. And seen from Moscow, this is basically what the entry of these States into NATO in its present form would mean. Let us beware. For Russia, this matter is most definitely a question of her vital national interests.

To see Poland integrated into an American political organization is, for Russia, to see its only real military rival stand at the gates of Ukraine. Ukraine would then become a zone of double influence. This is wholly unacceptable to Russia. On the other hand, once the European Union is recognized as an equal partner and ally of the United States, the situation will be quite different. It will then be possible to integrate countries such as Hungary and the Czech Republic into it. Not every nation will be able to gain entry; Poland and Romania may have to wait a long time to join. The complexity of their relations with Russia, her sensitivity with regard to neighboring territories (Moldova, Ukraine, Kaliningrad), and the intense feelings involved will long prevent Russia from taking such a risk. NATO's current expansion into Eastern Europe is a dangerous illusion. It will do nothing to heal the internal problems of the area. It might, in fact, precipitate a crisis that could accelerate Eastern Europe's disintegration.

Balancing the trans-Atlantic alliance is imperative. This relationship must become an equal partnership between the United States and Europe or it will not survive at all; it will fall apart completely in quarrels and concessions. The erosion of NATO's military strength and the overbearing attitude of the United States will outweigh all the old loyalties. At the beginning of the 1990s, France was alone in believing this. The United States' recent as well as present willingness to keep NATO going only as a way to make its influence dominate, while refusing to take on its responsibilities, have transformed the situation. The delays and the incoherent policy of the U.S. in Bosnia have disenchanted even its most faithful allies. It is now less necessary to plead the cause of a common European defense and more urgent to go ahead and build one.

It has become impossible to maintain two classes of countries within the European Union based whether or not they are members of NATO. This split between Europeans in the name of friendship with the United States flies in the face of common sense. It is inconceivable that countries that have chosen to build their future security together should remain divided in their relations to the United States for outdated historical reasons.

The future of our security is a blank slate. We must write upon it with one pen. Our task is to develop with the United States a relationship that is based not on the memory of the wars of the Europeans but on the reality of their union.

Bibliography

Numbers of entries correspond to the superscript numbers in the text.

GOVERNMENT AND INSTITUTIONAL SOURCES

1. Aspin, L. "From Deterrence to Denuking." Testimony before the Armed Services Committee, U.S. House of Representatives, January 21, 1992. U.S. Government Printing Office, Washington, DC, 1992.
2. Commission Justice et Paix. Report, "Les Forces Nucléaires en Europe." October 24, 1982.
3. Conférence Épiscopale [Bishops' Conference]. Paper, "Gagner la Paix." Paris, November 1983.
4. Cresson, E. Speech at the Institut des Hautes Etudes de Défense Nationale, Paris, September 7, 1989.
5. Documentation française. *Livre Blanc sur la Defense Nationale.* Documentation française, Paris, March 1994.
6. "Elargir la Dissuasion." "Un nouveau débat stratégique." Paris, Documentation française, December, 1992.
   a. paper by S. Ando, Italian Minister of Defense.
   b. paper by Indian Army Chief of Staff.
   c. paper by M. Rifkin, British Minister of Defence.
   d. paper by P. Joxe, French Minister of Defense.
   e. paper by G. Salamé, Director of Research of the Centre Nucléaire de Recherches Scientifiques.
7. Gergorin, J.-L. "Deterrence in the Post Cold War Era." Paper for the International Institute of Strategic Studies, September 15, 1991.
8. Institut Français de Recherches Internationales (IFRI). *Pacifisme et Dissuasion.* IFRI, Paris, 1983.
9. ———. Rapport Ramsès. IFRI, Paris, 1992.
10. Kissinger, H. "Nuclear Weapons and Foreign Policy," Council on Foreign Relations, New York, 1957.

11. Luttwak, E. "Point de vue américain sur la dissuasion, colloque sur un nouveau débat stratégique." Documentation française, Paris, December 1992.

12. McNamara, R. Speech in San Francisco, September 11, 1967.

13. Ministère des Affaires Etrangères—Centre d'Analyses et de Prévisions (MAE—CAP). "Quel avenir la dissuasion nucléaire?" MAE—CAP Paper. Paris, January 17, 1992.

14. Ministère des Affaires Etrangères—Direction Politique. "Le désarmement américano-russe et les forces tierces." Paper of MAE—Direction Politique. Paris, July 9, 1992.

15. ———. "La dissuasion minimale selon l'URSS." Paper of MAE—Direction Politique. Paris, October 4, 1991.

16. ———. "Le rôle des armes nucléaires en Europe," Paper of MAE—Direction Politique. Paris, February 9, 1992.

17. Mitterrand, F. Press conference. Aix-la-Chapelle, France, October 20, 1987.

18. ———. Press conference. Hanover, West Germany, October 22, 1987.

19. ———. Speech before the Institut des Hautes Etudes de Défense Nationale, October 11, 1988.

20. Rand Corporation Report, *Nuclear Weapons in a Changing World.* Rand Corporation, San Diego, CA, 1993:

    a. J. van Oudenaren (Rand), "Nuclear Weapons in the 90's and Beyond"

    b. N. Kapranov (IFSDH, Moscow). "A Russian Perspective"

    c. P. Williams (Pittsburg University), "Nuclear Weapons, European Security and Regional Deterrence"

    d. T. Enders et al. (Munich), "New Germany and Nuclear Weapons"

    e. S. Ogawa (National Institute for Defense Studies, Tokyo), "U.S. Nuclear Forces and Japanese Security."

    f. N. Kamal (Institute of Strategic Studies, Islamabad), "Proliferation in South-East Asia."

    g. S. Weber (University of California at Berkeley). "Security after the Revolutions of 89 and 91."

21. Schlesinger, J. U.S. *Department of Defense Annual Report.* Fiscal Year 1975.

22. SR/Bell Laboratories. "National Strategic Requirement for C3 to 1975." Final report. SR/Bell Laboratories, Stanford, CA, 1962.

23. Szabo, S. *West European Public Perceptions of Security Issues.* Office of Research, U.S. Information Agency, Washington, DC, July 1988.

24. U.S. Catholic Conference. "The Challenge of Peace, God's Promises, and Our Responses." U.S. Catholic Conference, 1983.

25. U.S. Government Printing Office. Testimony before the Foreign Relations/Foreign Affairs Committee, U.S. Congress, September 16, 1980. USGPO, Washington DC, 1980.
26. The World Bank, *World Development Report 1991.* The World Bank, Washington, DC, 1992.
27. ———. *World Development Report 1992.* The World Bank, Washington, DC, 1993.

JOURNALS AND PERIODICALS

28. Le Bourg, C. "Armée-Nation: la confiance." *Armées Aujourd'hui,* No. 128, March 1988.
29. *Asahi Shimbun,* June 21, 1975.
30. De Bresry, B. "Les Forces armées européennes en l'an 2000," *Défense nationale,* 1993.
31. *The European,* January 15, 1995.
32. *Far Eastern Economic Review,* April 25, 1995.
33. *Far Eastern Review,* December 15, 1994.
34. Wohlstetter, A. "The Delicate Balance of Terror." *Foreign Affairs,* January 1959.
35. Iklé, P. "Can Deterrence Last Out the Century?" *Foreign Affairs,* January 1973.
36. "Nuclear War Can Be Won," *Foreign Affairs,* Winter 1981.
37. McNamara R., Bundy, M., and Wenan, G. "The Future of Nuclear Weapons," *Foreign Affairs,* No. 4, Spring 1982.
38. Kayren, C., McNamara, R., and Rathjens, G. "Nuclear Weapons after the Cold War," *Foreign Affairs,* Autumn 1991.
39. Perry, W. "Desert Storm and Deterrence," *Foreign Affairs,* Autumn 1991.
40. *Foreign Affairs,* May/June, 1993.
41. Huntington, S. "The Clash of Civilizations." *Foreign Affairs,* Summer 1993.
42. *Foreign Affairs,* January/February 1995.
43. *Herald Tribune,* October 25, 1982.
44. Poll by the *Herald Tribune,* October 25, 1982.
45. *The Independent,* September 19, 1992.
46. Slocombe, W. "The Countervailing Strategy," *International Security,* Spring 1981.
47. Huntington, S. "Il est temps de voir les failles entre civilizations," *Libération,* September 23, 1993.

48. Howard, M. "La défense occidentale dans les années 80," *Politique étrangère,* No. 4, 1982.

49. Yost, D. "La dissuasion nucléaire en question." *Politique étrangère,* February 1990.

50. Hogan, M., and Smith, T. "Public Opinion and the Nuclear Freeze." *Public Opinion Quarterly,* Winter 1991.

51. Conze, H. and Picq, J. "L'avenir de la dissuasion nucléaire," *Revue de la Défense Nationale,* March 1993.

52. Géré, F. "Les quatre générations de l'apocalypse," *Stratégique,* January, 1992.

53. Poirier, L. "La crise des fondements," *Stratégique,* January 1992.

54. "European Executives Differ on Perception of Germany's Posture," *Wall Street Journal,* February 28, 1992.

55. "Germany Seeks to Mend Ties," *Wall Street Journal,* April 4, 1992.

56. Nan, H. "The Moral Argument for U.S. Leadership." *Wall Street Journal,* September 16, 1993.

57. *Wall Street Journal,* November 29, 1994.

BOOKS

58. Angell, N. *The Grand Illusion.* Thornton, London, 1912.

59. Asmus, R. D. *German Opinion after the Wall.* Rand Corporation, San Diego, CA, 1994.

60. *Atlaseco, 1994.* Editions du Sérail, Paris.

61. Attali, J. *Economie de l'Apocalypse.* Fayard, Paris, 1995.

62. Bellah, R. et al. *Habits of the Heart.* Harper & Row, New York, 1986.

63. Benedict, R. *Le Chrysanthème et le sabre.* Philippe Picquier, Arles, 1991.

64. Bobbit, P. "Selective Options and Limited Responses." *U.S. Nuclear Strategy,* Macmillan, London, 1989.

65. Churchill, W. *The World Crisis 1911–1914.* Thornton-Butterworth, London, 1923.

66. Cohen-Tannoudji, L. *L'Etat et la démocratie.* Odile Jacob, Paris, 1989.

67. Cohen-Tannoudji, L. *Le Droit sans état.* Odile Jacob, Paris, 1984.

68. De Closets, F. *Tant et plus.* Le Seuil/Grasset, Paris, 1992.

69. Doise, J. and Vaïsse, M. *Diplomatie et outil militaire.* Le Seuil, Paris, 1992.

70. Ehrlich, P., Sagan, C., et al. *Le Froid et les ténèbres.* Belfond, Paris, 1985.

71. Ford, D. *The Button. The Nuclear Trigger, Does It Work?* G. Allen and Unwin, Boston, 1985.

72. Friedman, G. and Lebond, M. *The Coming War with Japan.* St. Martin's Press, New York, 1993.

73. Gallois, P. *Stratégie de l'âge nucléaire.* Calmann-Lévy, Paris, 1960.

74. Glucksmann, A. *La Force du vertige.* Grasset, Paris, 1983.

75. Godement, F. *La Renaissance de l'Asie.* Odile Jacob, Paris, 1993.

76. Graham, T. *American Public Opinion on NATO, Deterrence and the Use of Nuclear Weapons.* Occasional Paper No. 4. University Press of America, Lanham, MD, 1989.

77. Guéhenno, J. -M. *La Fin de la démocratie.* Flammarion, Paris, 1993.

78. Guicherd, C. *L'Eglise catholique et la politique de défense au début des années 80.* Presses Universitaires de France, Paris, 1988.

79. Guicherd, C. *The Origins of Flexible Response.* Macmillan, London, 1988.

80. Hassner, P. *Écrire l'Histoire du XXe siècle.* Gallimard/Le Seuil, Paris, 1993.

81. Howard, M. *The Causes of War.* Unwin, London, 1983.

82. Hower-Dixon, T. "Environmental Changes and Violent Conflicts," *Scientific American,* February 1993.

83. Iklé, F. *Every War Must End.* Columbia University Press, New York, 1991.

84. Joxe, A. *Le Cycle de la dissuasion.* La Découverte, Paris, 1990.

85. Kennan, G., *The Nuclear Delusion.* Pantheon Books, New York, 1982.

86. Kepel, G., General Editor, *Les politiques de Dieu,* Le Seuil, Paris, 1993.

87. Kouchner, B. *Le Malheur des autres.* Odile Jacob, Paris, 1993.

88. Laïdi, Z., General Editor. *L'Ordre mondial relâché.* Éditions de la Fondation nationale des science politiques, Paris, 1992.

89. Laird, R. *France, The Soviet Union and the Nuclear Weapons Issue.* Westview Press, Boulder, CO, 1985.

90. Lellouche, P. *L'Avenir de la guerre.* Mazarine, Paris, 1985.

91. Lellouche, P. *Le Nouveau Monde.* Grasset, Paris, 1992.

92. Mansfield, ed. *Democratization and War.*

93. Manwaring, M. *Gray Area Phenomena.* Westview Press, Boulder, CO, 1993.

94. Migdal, J. S. *Strong Societies and Weak States.* Princeton University Press, Princeton, NJ, 1988.

95. *Monde-Europe, Rapport pour le XIème Plan,* Dunod, Paris, 1993.

96. National Science Foundation. *Science Indicators.* National Science Foundation, 1992.

97. Nolan, J. *Guardians of the Arsenals.* Basic Books, New York, 1989.

98. Nye, J., Jr. *Nuclear Ethics.* The Free Press, New York, 1986.

99. Parker, G. *La Révolution militaire.* Gallimard, Paris, 1993.

100. Poirier, L. *Des Stratégies nucléaires,* Hachette, Paris, 1988.

101. Poirier, L. *Théorie de la stratégie de dissuasion d'une puissance moyenne.* Hachette, Paris, 1968.

102. Roy, O. *L'Echec de l'Islam politique.* Le Seuil, Paris, 1992.

103. Roy, O., "La nouvelle donne 80–91," in Institut de Relations et Stratégiques/Cercle de réflexion et d'études sur les problèmes internationaux, ed., *Disparition et renaissance des empires au Moyen-Orient et en Asie centrale,* Dunod, Paris, 1992.

104. Ruffin, J. -C. *L'Empire et les nouveaux barbares.* Lattès, Paris, 1991.

105. Singer, J. -D. *Resort to Arms: International and Civil Wars 1816–1980.* Sage, Beverly Hills, CA, 1982.

106. Tetlock, P. and Lewis, R. *Behavior, Society and Nuclear War.* Oxford University Press, Oxford, 1989.

107. Thubron, C. *Derrière la Grande Muraille.* Payot, Paris, 1992.

108. *United States Strategic Bombing Survey.* Garland, New York, 1976.

109. Van Wolferen, K. *The Enigma of Japanese Power.* Vintage, New York, 1990.

110. Von Clausewitz, K. *De la Guerre.* Ivrea, Paris, 1989.